Screened Out

◆

Jean Baudrillard

Translated by Chris Turner

VERSO

London • New York

This edition first published by Verso 2002
© Verso 2002
Translation © Chris Turner 2002
First published as *Ecran total*
© Éditions Galilée 2000

1 3 5 7 9 10 8 6 4 2

Verso
UK: 6 Meard Street, London W1F 0EG
USA: 180 Varick Street, New York, NY 10014-4606
www.versobooks.com

Verso is the imprint of New Left Books

ISBN 1–85984–660–2
ISBN 1–85984–385–9 (pbk)

British Library Cataloguing in Publication Data
A catalogue record for this book is available from the British Library

Library of Congress Cataloging-in-Publication Data
A catalog record for this book is available from the Library of Congress

Typeset by M Rules
Printed at the Bath Press

History reproducing itself becomes farce
Farce reproducing itself becomes history

Contents

Translator's Foreword

With a few exceptions, these pieces originally appeared as articles in the Paris newspaper *Libération* between June 1987 and May 1997. The author made several minor changes in turning them into book form and a very few, even more minor rectifications have been made in preparing this translation.

The publication in book form contained no footnotes, some of the material initially published as such in the newspaper articles having been restored to the body of the text. The footnotes to this translation are therefore without exception my own and are included solely to elucidate points that would have been clear to a French audience at the time, but may be obscure to a non-French audience today.

C.T.

AIDS: Virulence or Prophylaxis?

AIDS, computer viruses, terrorism . . . Virulence makes its appearance when a body, system or network expels all its negative elements and resolves into a combinatorial of simple ones. In this sense, virality is closely related to fractality and digitality. It is because computers and electronic machines have become abstractions, virtual machines, non-bodies, that viruses run riot in them (they are much more vulnerable than traditional mechanical machines). It is because the body itself has become a non-body, an electronic, virtual machine, that viruses seize hold of it.

The current pathology of the body is now beyond the reach of conventional medicine, since it affects the body not as *form*, but as *formula*. The body of cancer is the body fallen victim to the disruption of its genetic formula. The AIDS body is the body damaged and impaired in its immune systems, in its systems of controls and anti-bodies.

These new pathologies are the illnesses of a codified, modelled body; they are sicknesses of the code and the model.

The human being, conceived as an electronic, cybernetic machine, makes a perfect home for viruses and viral illnesses, just as computers provide an ideal terrain for electronic viruses.

Here again, there is no effective prevention or therapy; the metastases invade the whole network 'virtually'; de-symbolized machine languages offer no more resistance to viruses than do de-symbolized bodies. The traditional mechanical accident or breakdown had a good old reparative medicine to deal with it, but the sudden failures, anomalies and 'betrayals' of anti-bodies (quite apart from any deliberate 'hacking' into their functions) are beyond remedy.

Virality is the pathology of closed circuits, of integrated circuits, of promiscuity and chain reactions. It is a pathology of incest, understood in a broad, metaphorical sense.

He who lives by the same will die by the same. The impossibility of exchange, of reciprocity, of alterity secretes that other invisible, diabolic, elusive alterity, that absolute Other, the virus, itself made up of simple elements and of recurrence to infinity.

We are in an incestuous society. And the fact that AIDS first hit the homosexual community and drug abusers has to do with this incestuousness of groups which function as closed circuits.

In the past, haemophilia struck at families with long histories of consanguine marriages, highly endogamous lineages. The strange disease which for a long time attacked cypress trees was a kind of virus which was in the end attributed to a reduction in the temperature differential between summer and winter, to the seasons coming to intermingle. There again, the spectre of the Self-same struck. In every compulsion for resemblance, every excision of differences, in every case of things being contiguous with their own images or becoming confused with their own code, there is a threat of incestuous virulence, of a diabolical alterity, knocking the marvellous machinery out of kilter. In other cases, this takes the form of the resurgence of the principle of Evil (there is no moral dimension or guilt here: the principle of Evil is merely synonymous with the principle of reversion and the principle of adversity). In systems moving towards total positivization – and hence de-symbolization – evil simply equates, in all its forms, with the fundamental rule of reversibility.

The uninterrupted production of positivity has a terrifying consequence: if negativity engenders crisis and critique, absolute positivity, for its part, engenders catastrophe, precisely through its incapacity to distil the crisis. Every structure, system or social body which ferrets out its negative, critical elements to expel them or exorcise them runs the risk of a catastrophe by total implosion and reversion, just as every biological body which hunts down and eliminates all its germs, bacillae and parasites – in short, all its biological enemies – runs the risk of cancer or, in other words, of a positivity devouring its own cells. It runs the risk of being devoured by its own anti-bodies, which now have nothing to do.

It is logical that AIDS (and cancer) should have become the prototypes for our modern pathology and for all lethal virality. When the body is exposed to artificial prostheses and, at the same time, to genetic fantasies, its defence systems are disorganized, its biological logic destroyed. This fractal body, fated to see its own external functions multiply, is at the same time doomed to unstoppable internal division among its own cells. It metastasizes: the internal, biological metastases are in a way symmetrical with those external metastases, the prostheses, the networks, the connections.

In an over-protected space, the body loses all its defences. We know that in operating theatres, there is such a level of prophylaxis that no microbe or bacteria can survive. Now, it is precisely there, in that absolutely spotless space that we are seeing mysterious, anomalous, viral diseases emerging. For viruses survive and proliferate as soon as room is made for them. So long as there were microbes, there were no viruses. In a world cleansed of its old infections, in an 'ideal' clinical world, an intangible, implacable pathology unfurls, a pathology born of disinfection itself.

A pathology of the third kind. Just as we are up against a new violence in our societies – a violence born of the paradox of a permissive and pacified society, so we are up against new diseases, the diseases of bodies over-protected by their artificial shields – both medical and computer shields. Bodies which are, as a result, susceptible to every virus, to the most 'perverse', unexpected chain reactions. A pathology no longer based in accidents or anomie, but in 'anomalies'. And it is the same in the social body, where the same causes produce the same perverse effects, the same unpredictable dysfunctions and a whole range of anomalies and terrorisms, comparable to the genetic disturbance of cells – a phenomenon similarly brought about by over-protection and over-coding. The social system, like the biological body, is losing its natural symbolic defences in direct proportion to the increased technological sophistication of its prostheses. And medicine is not going to find it easy to deal with this entirely new pathology, since it is itself part of the system of over-protection, the system of protectionist and prophylactic zeal towards the body. Just as there is apparently no political solution to the problem of terrorism, so there does not currently seem to be any biological solution to the problem of AIDS or cancer. And for the same reason: these are anomalous symptoms, a certain type of violence and certain types of illness arising from the depths of the system itself and countering, with reactive violence or virulence, the political over-control of the social body, the biological over-control of the physical body.

Yet this new form of virulence is ambiguous, and AIDS is an example of it. AIDS provides an argument for a new sexual prohibition, but it is no longer a *moral* prohibition: it is a functional prohibition on the circulation of sex. This breaks all the commandments of modernity. Sex, like money, like information, must circulate freely. Everything must be fluid, and acceleration is inevitable. To revoke sexuality on the grounds of a viral danger is as absurd as stopping international trade on the grounds that it is fuelling the cancerous rise of the dollar. No one seriously envisages such a thing. Now, at a stroke with AIDS: a stopping of sex. A contradiction in the system? Perhaps this suspension has some enigmatic purpose, linked contradictorily to the equally enigmatic purpose of sexual liberation?

The spontaneous self-regulation of systems is something well-known. We know how they produce accidents of their own, put a brake on their own operation, in order to survive on a basis contrary to their own principles. All societies survive *against* their own value-systems: they have to have such a system, but they also have to deny it and operate in opposition to it. Now, we live by at least two principles: the principle of sexual liberation and that of communication and information. But it is entirely as though the species were, through the AIDS threat, producing an antidote to its principle of sexual liberation, and, through cancer, which is a disruption of the genetic code and therefore a pathology of information, a resistance to the all-powerful principle of cybernetic control. What if all this signified a rejection of the obligatory flows of sperm, sex, signs and words, a rejection of forced communication, programmed information and sexual promiscuity? What if all this were a vital resistance to the expansion of flows, circuits and networks – admittedly, at the cost of a new lethal pathology, but a pathology which would in the end protect us from something even more serious? With AIDS and cancer, we might be said to be paying the price for our own system: we are exorcising its *banal* virulence in a *fatal* form.

No one can foretell how effective this exorcism will be, but we have to ask the question: what is it – what even worse eventuality (the total hegemony of the genetic code?) – that cancer is resisting? What is it – what even worse eventuality (a sexual epidemic, total sexual promiscuity?) – that AIDS is resisting? The drugs problem is the same: all dramatizing apart, we have to ask what it is protecting us from, what kind of escape route it represents from an even worse evil (rational stupefaction, normative sociability, universal regimentation). We may say the same of terrorism: isn't its secondary, reactional, abreactional violence protecting us from an epidemic of consensus, from a growing political leukaemia and deliquescence, and the invisible transparency of the State? Everything is ambiguous and reversible. After all, it is by neurosis that man protects himself most effectively from madness. In this sense, AIDS is not a punishment from on high; it might rather be a defensive emotional reaction of the species against the danger of a total promiscuity, a total loss of identity in the proliferation and acceleration of the networks.

If AIDS, terrorism, economic collapse and electronic viruses are concerns not just for the police, medicine, science and the experts, but for the entire collective imagination, this is because there is more to them than mere episodic events in an irrational world. They embody the entire logic of our system, and are merely, so to speak, the points at which that logic crystallizes spectacularly. Their power is a power of irradiation and their effect, through the media, within the imagination, is itself a viral one.

They are immanent phenomena which are all related to each other; they obey the same protocol of virulence and have contamination effects way beyond their actual impact. For example, a single terrorist act forces us to review the whole political dimension in the light of the terrorist hypothesis. The very emergence of AIDS, even at a statistically low level, forces us to review the whole spectrum of diseases and bodies in the light of the viral, immunodeficiency hypothesis. The tiniest little computer virus which degrades the Pentagon's memory banks or floods entire networks with Christmas greetings is enough to wreck the credibility of computer systems, and forces us to review all data with an eye to possible infiltration, calculated disinformation, risk and uncertainty. Which is not, objectively, without its funny side.

This is the privilege of extreme phenomena, and of catastrophe in general, since all these viral processes are clearly of the order of catastrophe (not in the moral sense, but as an anomalous way of things turning out). The secret order of catastrophe lies in the inseparability of all these contemporary processes – and, also, in the affinity of these eccentric phenomena with the banality of the whole system. All extreme phenomena are coherent with one another; they are so because they are coherent with the whole system.

This means it is no use looking to the rationality of the system to combat its excrescences. It is a total delusion to think extreme phenomena can be abolished. They will, rather, become increasingly extreme as our systems become increasingly sophisticated. And this is fortunate, since they are the cutting-edge therapy, the homeopathic therapy for those systems. Pitting Good against Evil no longer exists as a strategy. In transparent – homeostatic or homeofluid – systems, the only remaining strategy is that of Evil against Evil: the strategy of the greater evil. The only possible strategy is a fatal strategy. And this is not even a matter of choice: we can see it happening before our eyes. There is, then, a *homeopathic* virulence to AIDS, to stock market crashes, to computer viruses etc. Stock market crashes, terrorism, computer viruses, debt etc. are the part of the catastrophe which shows above the waterline. The other nine-tenths are submerged in virtuality.

The total catastrophe would be a situation in which all information was omnipresent, a state of total transparency – a state which is happily obscured in its effects by the computer virus. Thanks to that virus, we shall not race straight to the end of information and communication. That would be death. As an excrescence of this lethal transparency, the virus also serves as an alarm signal. It is rather like the acceleration of a fluid: it produces turbulence and anomalies which halt its course, or disperse it. Chaos serves as a limit to what would, otherwise, run off into the absolute void. So extreme phenomena serve, in their secret disorder, as prophylaxis-by-chaos against an extreme escalation of order and transparency. That catastrophe, the true catastrophe, does, thanks to them, remain virtual. If it did materialize, that would be the end. And indeed, in spite of them, we are already today seeing the beginning of the end of a certain thinking process. Similarly, in the case of sexual liberation, we are already seeing the beginning of the end of a certain process of *jouissance*. If total sexual promiscuity came about, it is sex itself which would be abolished in its asexual explosion. It is the same with stock market crashes and with trade. Speculation as extreme phenomenon, as turbulence, puts a stop on the total emancipation of real trading. By simulating the instantaneous ultra-circulation of value, by shorting out the economic model, it also shorts out the catastrophe that the free communication of all exchange would represent – this total liberation of trade being the true catastrophic moment of value.

In the face of this threat of total weightlessness, of an unbearable lightness of being, a universal promiscuity, a linearity of processes which would pitch us into the void, these sudden whirlwinds we call catastrophes are what keep us from catastrophe. These anomalies, these extreme phenomena recreate zones of gravitation and density which prevent things from dispersing totally. We may see this as our societies secreting their own particular form of 'accursed share', like those tribes which rid themselves of their excess population by suicidal plunges into the ocean – a homeopathic suicide of some of their members which preserved the homeostatic balance of the whole.

Catastrophe reveals itself, then, to be a well-tempered strategy of the species. Or, rather, our viruses, our extreme phenomena – very real, but localized – would seem to enable us to maintain intact the energy of virtual catastrophe, which is the engine driving all our processes – in the economy, in politics, in the arts and in history. And isn't energy itself, in its concept, a form of *catastrophe*?

1 June 1987

We are all Transsexuals Now

It is interesting to track the changes in the sexed body, exposed as it is today to a kind of artificial fate. And that artificial fate is transsexuality. An artificial fate not in the sense of a deviation from the natural order, but insofar as it is the product of a change in the symbolic order of sexual difference. And transsexual not (just) in the sense of anatomical sexual transformation, but in the wider sense of transvestism – of playing on interchangeable signs of sex, and, by contrast with the previous play on sexual difference, of *playing on sexual indifference*.

Indifference in two senses: the transsexual is both a play on non-differentiation (of the two poles of sexuality) and a form of indifference to *jouissance*, to sex as *jouissance*. The sexual has *jouissance* as its focus (*jouissance* is the leitmotif of sexual liberation), whereas the transsexual tends towards artifice – both the anatomical artifice of changing sex and the play on vestimentary, morphological and gestural signs characteristic of cross-dressers. In both cases – surgical or semiurgical operation, sign or organ – what is involved is prosthetics and today, when it is the body's destiny to become a prosthesis, it is logical that the model of sexuality should become transsexuality and that transsexuality should everywhere become the site of seduction.

We are all transsexuals. Just as we are all potential biological mutants, so we are all also potential transsexuals. And this is not even a matter of biology. We are all *symbolically* transsexuals.

Take La Cicciolina.[1] Is there any more wonderful embodiment of sex, of the pornographic innocence of sex? She has been contrasted with Madonna, the virgin product of aerobics and a glacial aesthetic, devoid of all charm and sensuality, a muscled android, ripe for precisely that reason for conversion into a computer-generated idol on account of the strange deterrence she generates. But, if we think about it, is not La Cicciolina also a transsexual? Her long, platinum-blonde hair, her ample, pneumatic breasts, her ideal blow-up-doll forms, her lyophilized-cartoon or science-fiction eroticism and, above all, the exaggeration of the sexual discourse (never perverse, never libertine), total transgression on a plate; the ideal telephone chat-line woman, plus a carnivorous erotic ideology which no woman today would sign up to − except, precisely, a transsexual, a transvestite: they alone, as we know, live by the exaggerated, carnivorous signs of sexuality. Here, that fleshly ectoplasm La Cicciolina meets the artificial nitroglycerine of Madonna or the androgynous, Frankenstinian charm of Michael Jackson. They are all mutants, transvestites, genetically baroque beings, whose erotic 'look' conceals their gender indeterminacy. They are all 'gender-benders', as they say in the USA.

In reality, the myth of sexual liberation is still alive in many forms, but, in the imaginary register, the transsexual myth − with its androgynous, hermaphroditic variants − is dominant. After the orgy, desire and sexual difference, we have here the flourishing of erotic simulacra of all kinds and transsexual kitsch in all its glory. Postmodern pornography, so to speak, in which sexuality gets lost in the theatrical

1. The Hungarian-born porn star Ilona Staller, who went on to become an Italian member of parliament on an anti-nuclear, pro-sexual freedom platform.

excess of its ambiguity and indifference. Things have certainly changed since sex and politics were part of the same subversive project: if La Cicciolina can be elected to the Italian Parliament now, that is precisely because the transsexual and the transpolitical meet in the same ironic indifference. This particular feat, which would have been unthinkable just a few years ago, but which today meets with warm general approval, attests to the fact that it is not just sexual culture, but the whole of the political culture that has gone over to transvestism.

The strategy of exorcizing the sexual body by wildly exaggerating the signs of sex, of exorcizing desire by its secret depolarization and the exaggeration of its *mise en scène*, is much more effective than that of good old repression, which, by contrast, used prohibition to create difference. Yet it is not clear who benefits from this strategy, as everyone suffers it without distinction. This travestied regime – in the broadest sense – has become the very basis of our institutions. You find it everywhere – in politics, architecture, theory, ideology and even in science.

You even find it in our desperate quest for identity and difference. We no longer have the time to seek out an identity in the historical record, in memory, in a past, nor indeed in a project or a future. We have to have an instant memory which we can plug in to immediately – a kind of promotional identity which can be verified at every moment. What we look for today, where the body is concerned, is not so much health, which is a state of organic equilibrium, but fitness, which is an ephemeral, hygienic, promotional radiance of the body – much more a performance than an ideal state – which turns sickness into failure. In terms of fashion and appearance, we no longer pursue beauty or seductiveness, but the 'look'.

Everyone is after their 'look'. Since you can no longer set any store by your own existence (we no longer look at each other – and seduction is at an end!), all that remains is to perform *an appearing act*, without bothering to *be*, or even to be seen. It is not: 'I exist, I'm here', but 'I'm visible, I'm image – look, look!' This is not even narcissism. It's a depthless extraversion, a kind of promotional ingenuousness in which everyone becomes the impresario of his/her own appearance.

The 'look' is a kind of minimal, low-definition image, like the video image or, as McLuhan would say, a tactile image, which provokes neither attention nor admiration, as fashion still does, but is a pure special effect without any particular meaning. The look is not exactly fashion any more; it is a form of fashion which has passed beyond. It no longer subscribes to a logic of distinction and it is no longer a play of difference; it plays at difference without believing in it. It is indifference. Being oneself becomes an ephemeral performance, with no lasting effects, a disenchanted mannerism in a world without manners.

Retrospectively, this triumph of the transsexual and the travestied casts a strange light on the sexual liberation of earlier generations. That liberation, far from being, as in its own self-image, the irruption of a maximum erotic value of the body – with an elevation of the feminine and *jouissance* (the masculine having rather reserved for itself up to that point the field of power) – will perhaps merely have been an intermediate phase on the path to gender confusion. The sexual revolution will perhaps merely have been a decisive stage in the journey towards transsexuality. This is, ultimately, the problematic fate of every revolution. By releasing all the potentialities of desire, the sexual revolution leads to the basic question: am I man or woman? (psychoanalysis has at least played a part in generating this sexual uncertainty principle). As for the political and social revolution – the prototype for all the others – by giving human beings the use of their freedom and their own free will, it will have led them, in an implacably logical process, to wonder where their free will lies, what they ultimately want and what they are entitled to expect of themselves – a problem previously quite unknown. This is the paradoxical outcome of every revolution. With revolution begins indeterminacy, anxiety and confusion, but many other pleasures too: choice, pluralism, democracy.

But there simply is no democratic principle of sexuality. Sex is not part of human rights and there is no principle of the emancipation of sexuality. Once the orgy was over, sexual liberation could be seen to have had the effect of leaving everyone searching for their gender, their sexual and gender identity, with fewer and fewer possible answers, given the circulation of signs and the multiplicity of pleasures. This is how we subtly became transsexuals, just as we secretly became transpolitical – that is to say, politically indifferent and undifferentiated beings, politically androgynous and hermaphroditic. Having subscribed to, digested and rejected the most contradictory ideologies, we now merely wear the masks and have become in our minds, perhaps unwittingly, political cross-dressers.

What other things do we see simultaneously gaining the upper hand? Terrorism as (transpolitical) political form, AIDS and cancer as pathological form, the trans-sexual and the travestied as sexual and aesthetic form in general. Only these forms provide any genuine mental fascination today. Neither the sexual revolution nor the political debate, neither cardiovascular disease nor accidents at work, nor even conventional warfare, interest anyone collectively any more (this is a good thing where war is concerned; we shall have been spared many wars because they would have been of no interest to anyone). The true phantasms lie elsewhere. They lie in these three forms, all of them products of the disturbance of a principle of functioning and the resultant confusion of effects, and each of them (terrorism, transvestism, AIDS) corresponding to an exacerbation of the political, sexual or genetic game, as well as to a defectiveness and collapse of the respective codes of the political and sexual spheres.

They are all viral, fascinating, indifferent forms, forms multiplied by the virulence of images, since all the modern media – the information and communications systems – have themselves a viral power and their virulence is contagious. We are in a culture where bodies and minds are irradiated by signals and images and, though that culture produces the finest effects, it comes as no surprise that it also produces the most lethal viruses. The nuclearization of bodies began at Hiroshima, but it continues endemically, incessantly, in irradiation by the media, by images, signs, programmes and networks.

14 October 1987

Necrospective around
Martin Heidegger

The futile quarrel over Heidegger has no specific meaning within philosophy. It is merely symptomatic of a weakness in current thinking. Unable to find any new energy, philosophical thought keeps going back obsessively over its origins, over the purity of its references; it is now painfully reliving, in this *fin de siècle* period, its own primal scene of the early part of the century. More generally, the Heidegger case is symptomatic of the collective vogue for revivals which has taken hold of this society as it begins its end-of-century stock-taking: a revival of Nazism, fascism and the holocaust. The same temptation to re-examine the century's historical primal scene is at work here, a temptation to 'launder' the corpses and clean up the historical record, but at the same time there is also in all this a perverse fascination with a return to the wellsprings of violence, a collective attempt to hallucinate the historical truth of evil. Our present imagination must be weak indeed and our indifference to our own situation and our own philosophizing very great for us to need such regressive magic.

In the case of Heidegger we are suddenly discovering his act of intellectual treachery (if such it was) today, even though we have lived quite happily with it for forty years. We saw the same thing happen with Marx and Freud. When Marxist thought lost its triumphal aura, people started ferreting about in Marx's life and discovered that he was a bourgeois who slept with his maid. When psychoanalytic thought began to lose its uncontested influence, people began looking into Freud's own life and psychology and, inevitably, found he was sexist and patriarchal. Now we have Heidegger accused of being a Nazi.

The fact that he has been so accused and that efforts are being made to prove his innocence is really of no consequence: both parties to the quarrel have fallen into the same petty-minded intellectual trap, the trap of an enervated form of thinking which no longer even takes pride in its own basic tenets, nor has the energy to go beyond them, and which is squandering what energy it still possesses in historical trials, accusations, justifications and verifications. This is the self-defence of the philosophical world casting a suspicious eye on the dubious morals of its masters (if not, indeed, trampling them down as 'master-thinkers'). It is the self-defence of an entire society which is unable to generate a new history and is hence condemned to keep on re-hashing past history to prove its own existence, or even to prove its own crimes.

But what are we trying to prove? It is because we have disappeared *today* politically and historically (this is our real problem) that we want to prove we actually died between 1940 and 1945 at Auschwitz or Hiroshima – that at least is a kind of history that really has some weight to it. In this we are behaving just like the Armenians who never stop trying to prove they were massacred in 1917; an inaccessible, useless proof, but one which is vital to them in a way. It is because philosophy today has disappeared (that is its problem: how can it live on in a state of disappearance?) that it has to prove that it was definitively compromised by what Heidegger did or rendered aphasic by Auschwitz. What is happening, then, is a desperate attempt to snatch a posthumous truth from history, a posthumous exculpation – and this at a moment when there is precisely not enough truth around to allow us to arrive at any sort of verification, nor enough philosophy to ground any relation whatever between theory and practice, nor enough history to produce any kind of historical proof of what happened.

We tend all too easily to forget that our reality comes to us through the media, the tragic events of the past included. This means that it is too late to verify and understand them historically, for precisely what characterizes our century's end is the fact that the tools of historical intelligibility have disappeared. History had to be understood while there still was history. Heidegger should have been denounced (or defended) while there still was time. A trial can only be conducted when there is some way for justice to be done afterwards. It is too late now; we have been moved on to other things, as we saw when *Holocaust* was shown on television, and even when *Shoah* was screened. Those phenomena were not understood at the time when we still had the means to understand them. They will not be understood now. This is so because such fundamental notions as responsibility, objective cause and the meaning (or non-meaning) of history have already disappeared or are disappearing. The effects of moral conscience, or collective conscience, are entirely media effects, and you can see from the extraordinary therapeutic effort being made to resuscitate that conscience how little life is left in it.

We shall never know whether Nazism, the concentration camps or Hiroshima were intelligible or not. We are no longer in the same mental universe. The reversibility of victim and victimizer, the diffraction and dissolution of responsibility – these are the virtues of our marvellous interface today. We no longer have the strength to forget; our amnesia is the amnesia of images. Amnesties seem impossible: since everyone is guilty, who could declare one? As for autopsies, no one believes in the anatomical veracity of facts any more. We work on models. Even if the facts were there staring us in the face, we would not be convinced.

Thus the more we have pored over Nazism and the gas chambers in an effort to analyse those things, the less intelligible they have become, and we have in the end arrived quite logically at the improbable question: 'When it comes down to it, did all these things really exist?' The question may be stupid or morally indefensible, but what is interesting is what makes it logically *possible* to ask it. And what makes it possible is the way the media have substituted themselves for events, ideas and history. This means that the longer you examine these phenomena, the more you master all the details to identify their causes, the more their existence fades and the more they come to have not existed at all: a confusion over the identity of things induced by the very act of investigating and memorizing them. An indifference of memory, an indifference to history that is exactly equal to the very efforts made to objectify it. One day we shall ask ourselves if Heidegger himself really existed. Faurisson's paradox[2] may seem abominable – and, insofar as he claims that the gas chambers did not exist historically, it *is* abominable – but in a sense it exactly expresses the situation of an entire culture: the dead-end that our *fin-de-siècle* society has got itself into, fascinated as it is to the point of distraction by the horror of its own origins. Since it is impossible to forget those origins, the only way out is denial.

If proof is futile here, as there is no historical discourse in which to conduct a trial, punishment is also impossible. Nothing can atone for Auschwitz and the holocaust. There is no possible way of fitting the punishment to the crime, and the unreality of a possible punishment makes the facts themselves seem unreal. What we are living through has nothing to do with all this. What is happening right now, collectively, confusedly, in all these trials and polemics is the transition from the

2. Robert Faurisson, formerly a professor at the University of Lyon is the most prominent of France's 'revisionist' historians.

phase of history to a phase of myth. We are seeing the mythic reconstruction, the media reconstruction, of all these events. And in a sense this mythic conversion is the only operation which can, if not perhaps morally exculpate us, at least absolve us in fantasy of responsibility for this original crime. But before this process can take place, before a crime can become a myth, the crime has first to be divested of its historical reality. Otherwise, since we have been, and still are, unable to come to terms historically with all these things – fascism, concentration camps, the holocaust – we would be condemned to repeat them eternally as a primal scene.

It is not nostalgia for fascism which is dangerous. What is dangerous and lamentable is this pathological revival of the past, in which everyone – both those who deny and those who assert the reality of the gas chambers, both Heidegger's critics and his supporters – is currently participating (indeed virtually conniving), this collective hallucination which transfers the power of imagination that is lacking from our own period, and all the burden of violence and reality which has today become merely illusory, back to that earlier period in a sort of compulsion to relive its history, a compulsion accompanied by a profound sense of guilt at not having been there. All this is a desperate emotional response to the realization that the events in question are currently eluding us at the level of reality. The Heidegger affair, the Barbie trial etc. are the pathetic little convulsions produced by the loss of reality that afflicts us today, and Faurisson's propositions are simply the cynical transposition of that loss of reality into the past. Faurisson's 'none of this ever existed' quite simply means that we do not even exist enough today to sustain a memory, and that all that remains to give us a sense of being alive are the techniques of hallucination.

Postscript: in view of all this, could we not just skip the rest of the century? I intend to launch a collective petition (which will make a change from the usual humanitarian or presidential petitions) calling for the 1990s to be cancelled, so that we can move directly from 1989 to the year 2000. As the *fin-de-siècle* has already arrived, with all its necrocultural pathos, its endless lamentations, commemorations and mummifications, do we really have to spend another ten boring years on this same old treadmill?

27 January 1988

In Praise of a Virtual Crash

The interesting element in the tragicomedy on the stock exchanges in recent months is the uncertainty as to whether a catastrophe has occurred. Has there been a 'real' catastrophe? Will there be one? The answer is: the catastrophe is a virtual one, and there will be no real catastrophe because we live under the sign of virtual catastrophe. This is connected with a state of affairs which was shown up strikingly here: the discrepancy between the fictional economy and the real economy. It is this discrepancy which protects us from a real catastrophe of the productive economies. Is this a good or a bad thing? It is exactly the same as the discrepancy between orbital war and land wars. Land wars go on everywhere, but nuclear war has not broken out. If the two were not disconnected, the nuclear confrontation would have erupted long since. We are dominated by bombs and virtual catastrophes which do not explode: the international stock market crash (this has not really eventuated and it will not), nuclear war, the third-world debt, and even the demographic time-bomb. One could, of course, argue that all these things will inevitably blow up in our faces one day, just as there has long been a prediction that, within the next fifty years, an earthquake will surely see California slide into the Pacific.

But the facts are clear: we are in the situation where the catastrophe does not eventuate, in a situation of virtual catastrophe – *eternally* virtual catastrophe.

This is how things are for us; it is the only reality objectively facing us: a wild, orbital round-dance of capital which, when it breaks down, produces no substantial disequilibrium in real economies (unlike the 1929 Crash, when the fictional and the real economies were by no means as disconnected, and, as a result, the catastrophe within the one had an impact on the other), either because real economies are themselves so speculative that they absorb more easily today what they could not absorb in 1929, or because the sphere of virtual capital has become so autonomous, so orbitalized, that it can in some cases proliferate – or even devour itself – without leaving any trace. It does, however, leave at least one catastrophic trace: the crash that has occurred has been not so much in the economy as in economic theory, which is now at a total loss before this explosion of its object. For everything has become a problem of communication. In the orbital sphere of capital, there is wonderfully good communication (the perverse computers and the 'golden boys', who are themselves human computing machines). This is the reason why it is in a permanently catastrophic state: the communications are too good. On the other hand, between the two spheres (of the virtual and the real), there is no longer any communication. Fortunately or otherwise. For it is this break between the two, this loss of a referent on the part of the virtual economy, which enables it to produce prodigious effects, but it is also this which protects the real economy from the catastrophes which may occur in the other sphere. Would it be better if the real economy became the referent and criterion for the fictional economy (every economist's dream)? There is little indication that it would, and in any case it is unthinkable.

Traditional theorists of war must be equally at a loss before the explosion of their object of study. For, paradoxically, it isn't the bomb which has exploded, but the war-object, which has exploded into two separate parts – a total, virtual war in orbit and multiple real wars on the ground. The two have neither the same dimensions nor the same rules, just as the virtual economy and the real economy do not have the same dimensions or the same rules. We shall have to get used to this virtually definitive division, accustom ourselves to a world dominated by this discrepancy. There was, admittedly, a crisis in 1929, and an explosion at Hiroshima, and hence there was a moment when these two worlds explosively contaminated each other, a moment when the economic slump and nuclear warfare were real, but we should not be misled by this as to what was to follow. Capital has not lurched from one crisis to another, each worse than the last (as Marx argued it would), nor have we lurched from one war to another. The event took place once and that is all. What came after was something quite different: it was the hyper-realization of big finance capital, the hyper-realization of overkill capacity, both orbitalized above our heads on a course quite beyond our grasp, and a course which is, fortunately, also beyond the grasp of reality itself. Hyper-realized war and hyper-realized money circulate in an inaccessible space, but in doing so they leave the world just as it is. In the end, the economies continue to produce, whereas the tiniest logical consequence of the fluctuations in the fictional economy would long ago have sufficed to wipe them out (let us not forget that in the daily figures for international trade, only 100 billion dollars goes on commercial transactions, while capital movements stand at 900 billion). The world continues to exist, even though one thousandth of the available nuclear power would have been enough to annihilate it; the Third World – and the other – survive even though the slightest inclination to meet its debt would already have wiped it from the map. Instead, that debt has begun to put itself into orbit; it is beginning to circulate from one bank to another, one country to another, each buying it back from the others. In this way it will eventually be forgotten, as it is sent into orbit with nuclear waste and a great many other things.

When the debt becomes too burdensome we expel it into a virtual space, where it appears as a catastrophe frozen in orbit. The debt becomes a satellite of the earth, just as war has become a satellite of the earth, just as the billions of dollars of speculative capital have become a satellite-heap, revolving endlessly around the planet. And it is, no doubt, better that it should be that way. While they are revolving – and even if they explode in space (as the billions 'lost' in the 1987 crash did) – the world is not changed by them, and this is the best we can hope for. The 'rational' hope of reconciling the fictional and real economies is entirely utopian: these billions of dollars exist only virtually; they cannot be transposed into the real economy. And a good thing too, for if they could by some miracle be re-injected into the production economies, that would spell real catastrophe. Similarly, we definitely should not try to re-connect the two separate spheres of warfare: let us leave virtual war in orbit, since that is where it protects us. In its very abstraction, its monstrous eccentricity, the nuclear is our best protection. And let us get used to living in the shade of these monstrous excrescences: the orbital bomb, financial speculation, the world debt, over-population (for which no orbital solution has yet been found – perhaps here again it will lie in the eccentric mobilization and circulation of the excess). As they are, they exorcize themselves in their excess, in their very hyperreality, and, after a fashion, leave the world intact, leave it free of its double.

The end of political economy is a thing we dreamed of with Marx. It was a dream in which classes died out and the social sphere became transparent, in accordance with an ineluctable logic of the crisis of capital. Then we dreamed the dream against Marx himself, disavowing the postulates of economics. A radical alternative this, denying any primacy to the economic or political spheres in first or last instance: political economy quite simply abolished as epiphenomenon, vanquished by its own simulacrum and by a higher logic. We no longer even need to dream of that end today. Political economy is disappearing by its own hand before our very eyes; it is turning into a transeconomics of speculation and flouting its own logic (the law of value, of the market, production, surplus-value, the very logic of capital), as it develops into a game with floating, arbitrary rules, a *jeu de catastrophe*. Political economy will have come to an end, but not at all as we expected it to – it will have ended by becoming exacerbated to the point of parody. Speculation is no longer surplus-value; it is the ecstasy of value, without reference to production or its real conditions. It is the pure and empty form, the expurgated form of value, which plays now on its own orbital circulation and revolution alone. It is by destabilizing itself monstrously, ironically, as it were, that political economy short-circuits every alternative. For what can you set against such an upping of the stakes, which in its own way takes over the energy of potlatch, of poker, of the challenge to its own logic, and represents, as it were, the transition to the aesthetic and frenzied phase of the economy – a way of putting an end to the economy that is the most singular in style, ultimately more original than our political utopias? Faced with this dangerous leap, can theory make a double leap to maintain its advantage?

2 March 1988

The Viral Economy

AIDS, the stock market crash (followed by the dawn raiders and a string of takeover bids), computer viruses – we are having more than our fair share of 'superconductive' events. More than our fair share of these sudden intercontinental ravages which no longer affect states, individuals or institutions, but entire structures, structures running right across society: sex, money, information and communications.

The three things are not interchangeable, but there is a family resemblance between them. AIDS is a kind of collapse of the sexual market, and we ought not to forget that computers, themselves affected with a kind of AIDS today, played a 'virulent' role in the Wall Street Crash. But the galloping contamination of computers could also be seen as akin to a devastating fall in the stock of computing. Contagion is not merely active *within* each system; it operates *between* systems.

All these developments have a generic pattern to them: the pattern of catastrophe. Admittedly, signs of this virulence and disruption have long been present in each of these systems: AIDS is now endemic; financial collapse, prefigured in the famous Wall Street Crash of 1929, is always a risk if panic sets in on the markets;

and hacking (and serial electronic accidents) go back at least twenty years. But the fact of all these endemic forms appearing together – and being almost simultaneously ratcheted up to a virulent state, a state of galloping anomaly – creates an entirely original, exciting situation. The effects are not necessarily of the same order in the collective consciousness: AIDS may be experienced as a real catastrophe; the stock market crash, by contrast, seems a *jeu de catastrophe*, and as for the computer virus, that is, admittedly, dramatic in its virtual consequences, but at the same time it is hilariously ironic. It is, in a sense, a catastrophic parody. The contagion of computer viruses is also the contagion of laughter (laughter is a form of contagion born of the catastrophic collapse of the real – even an infinitesimally tiny collapse; laughter is a homeopathic catastrophe). And the sudden epidemic which is striking down computers, destroying their defence and immune systems, can be a source of justified rejoicing – at least in the imagination (though not for the professionals concerned).

To these various aspects of a single eccentric cluster of phenomena, I shall add two very different things, though they inevitably put us in mind of the same mechanisms. The first is art, which is everywhere beset by questions of falsehood, authenticity, copying, cloning and simulation (there is a positive contagion here, destabilizing aesthetic values, which are also losing their immune defences) and simultaneously by a mad, speculative upward spiral of prices (though the art 'market' is no longer a market, but a centrifugal proliferation of value, in every way equivalent to the secondary infections of a body irradiated by lucre).

The second phenomenon is a political one: terrorism. Nothing more resembles the chain reaction of terrorism in our irradiated societies (irradiated by what? By superfusion of happiness, security, information and communication; by the disintegration of core symbols, fundamental rules, social contracts? – who knows?) than the chain reaction of AIDS, the dawn raiders, or the hackers. And the contagion of terrorism is as locally-confined, ephemeral, enigmatic and irrepressible as the contagion of all these phenomena. Hostage-taking is contagious too: when a software engineer puts a 'soft bomb' into the programme, using the possible destruction of that programme as a means of exerting pressure, what is he doing but taking the programme and all its future users hostage? And what do dawn raiders do but take – and hold – companies hostage, speculating on their death or resurrection on the stock market? We may say, then, that all the effects described operate on the same model as terrorism (hostages have a market price like shares or paintings), with the same Dutch auction going on, the same unpredictability, the same destabilization and chain-reaction effects. But we could just as well see terrorism on the model of AIDS, computer viruses or hostile takeover bids: none of these phenomena takes precedence over the others; there is no process of cause and effect here; it is a single constellation of collusive, contemporary phenomena.

The stock market crash finds a continuation in the takeover frenzy. It is no longer stocks and shares being bought, but companies being bought up. A virtual effervescence is created, with a potential impact on economic restructuring which, in spite of what is said, is purely speculative. The hope is that this enforced circulation will produce a broker's commission – exactly as on the Stock Exchange. Not even an objective profit exactly: the profit from speculation is not exactly surplus-value, and what is at stake here is certainly not what is at stake in classical capitalism. Speculation, like poker or roulette, has its own runaway logic, a chain-reaction logic, a process of intensification [*Steigerung*], in which the thrill of the game and of bidding up the stakes plays a considerable role. This is why there is no point criticizing it on the basis of economic logic (this is what makes these phenomena so exciting: the economic being overtaken by a random, vertiginous form).

The game is such as to become suicidal: big companies end up buying back their own shares, which is nonsensical from the economic point of view: they end up mounting takeover bids for themselves! But this is all part of the same madness. In the case of takeovers, companies are not traded – do not circulate – as real capital, as units of production; they are traded as a quantity of shares, as a mere probability of production, which is enough to create a virtual movement within the economy. That this will be a prelude to other crashes is highly probable, for the same reasons as apply in the case of stocks and shares: things are circulating too quickly. We might imagine labour itself – labour power – moving into this speculative orbit too. The worker would no longer sell his labour power for a wage, as in the classic capitalist process, but sell his job itself, his employment. And he would buy others and sell them on again, as their stock went up or down on the Labour Exchange (the term would then assume its full meaning). It would not be so much a question of doing the jobs as keeping them circulating, creating a virtual movement of employment which substituted for the real movement of labour.

Science fiction? Hardly. Information and communication are based on the principle of a value which has ceased to be referential and is now based on pure circulation. Pure added-value – added by dint of the message, the meaning passing from image to image and screen to screen. This is no longer even the surplus-value and exchange-value of the commodity (which does, however, anticipate this process). That is based in principle on a use-value and hence still belongs to the sphere of the economy. Here there is no longer any exchange properly speaking: we are in the realm of pure circulation and chain reactions through the networks: a whole new definition of value as something purely centrifugal, linked to pure speed and intensified exchange. This is largely what we see in the communications and information field – a field of virtuality; operational, but never operative.

But this 'transeconomic' model of value already exists in a sense in primitive cultures. For example, *kula* is a cycle of gift-exchange in which the gifts acquire increasing value the more they have been given and received.[3] They can even return to the starting point without having changed, but with their value enhanced a hundredfold (isn't it the same on today's art market?). The mere fact of passing from one person to another creates a kind of symbolic circulation energy, which transmutes into value. But that value cannot be realized. It cannot be 'produced', nor can it be transferred into the circuit of useful values (*gimwali*); it can only circulate indefinitely, increasing as exchanges occur (or, possibly, collapsing if they stop). Now *kula* is, in a sense, the sacred level, the prestige level of (symbolic) exchange. The other level, the level of barter, of equivalence, has no symbolic value; it is functional. *Potlatch* too is a speculative structure of outbidding, of production of value by purely and simply bidding up the price.

Can we say, then, that there is an echo of *kula* and *potlatch* in these wayward effects, which basically contradict the economic principle of value and equivalence, the principle of labour and production? In all logic (even in the logic of radical critique), we could not condemn these excesses. And everyone enjoys them as spectacle: the stock market, the art market, the Wall Street raiders. We all delight in these things as part of capital's spectacular brightening of our lives, its mania for the aesthetic. At the same time we delight – with more difficulty and more pain, and more ambiguously – in the spectacular pathology of that system, in the viruses which, like AIDS, the stock market crash and computer viruses, latch on to this delicate machinery and knock it out of kilter. But they are in fact following out the same logic: viruses and virulence are part of the logical, hyperlogical coherence of all our systems; they take the same paths and even create some new ones (computer viruses explore marginal areas of the networks which even

---

3. On the *kula* system, see Marcel Mauss, *The Gift. The Form and Reason for Exchange in Archaic Societies* (New York/London: W. W. Norton, 2000), pp. 21–31.

the networks had not planned to use). Computer viruses are an expression of the lethal transparency of information throughout the world. AIDS is an emanation of the lethal transparency of sexual liberation on a scale affecting entire social groups. Financial crashes are an expression of the lethal transparency of economies one to another, of the fulgurating circulation of values, which is the very basis of the liberation of production and exchange. Once they have been 'liberated', all these processes enter a supercooled state, the French term chiming felicitously here with notions of fusion and meltdown. This supercooling of event processes which become decoupled from their real substance is one of the great attractions of our age.[4]

And it is quite some paradox to see the economy coming triumphantly back on to the agenda, including the media agenda (let us not forget that the world of the media is a viral world too, and that the circulation of images and messages functions as a perpetual rumour mill). But can we still speak of the 'economy'? Or, indeed, of political economy (the logic of capital)? Certainly not. At the very least, the striking prominence of the economy at the moment has not at all the same meaning it had in the classical or Marxist analysis. For it is no longer in any sense driven by the infrastructure of material production, nor indeed by the superstructure. The engine of the economy is the destructuring of value, the destabilizing of markets and real economies, the triumph of an economy relieved of ideologies, social sciences, history and political economy and yielded up to pure speculation; it is the triumph of a virtual economy relieved of real economies (not really, of course, but virtually: yet it is not reality which holds sway today but virtuality); the triumph of a viral economy which connects up in this way with all the other viral processes. It

---

4. Baudrillard is here exploiting the term *surfusion* ('supercooling' or 'undercooling') for its poetic resources. This is also 'surfusion' as an excess of, a beyond of, 'fusion'.

is as an arena of special effects, of unpredictable (almost meteorological) happenings — as the destruction and exacerbation of its own logic — that it is becoming once again a kind of exemplary theatre of current events.

9 November 1988

The Depressurization of the West

With the Rushdie affair, Khomeini can be said to have opened up a new era in the history of hostage-taking. The awkward part in hostage-taking, as is well known, is storing and keeping the hostage. Khomeini has pulled off the brilliant trick of having the Western powers themselves detain and stand guard over the hostage. And, through Rushdie, he has pulled off the brilliant trick of having the West as a whole take itself hostage. This spectacular enhancement of hostage-taking strategy has turned it into something global – a symbolic strategy capable of overturning all relations of force merely by opening one's mouth.

Instead of talking a lot of nonsense about the Ayatollah's medieval barbarity and hoping the whole thing will disappear miraculously with his death, it would be better to ponder why an act of this kind has such symbolic potency, why it is so symbolically – diabolically – effective.

After an exhausting war and in an entirely negative political, military and economic situation, with the whole world united against him, the Ayatollah has a single, tiny, immaterial weapon at his disposal. But it is close to being the absolute weapon: the principle of Evil. A position of absolute disavowal of the Western values of progress, rationality, political morality, democracy, etc. Denying the universal consensus on all these fine things confers on him the whole energy of Evil – all the satanic energy of the outcast, the *éclat* of the accursed share. He alone speaks today, because he alone, against all comers, has taken up the Manichean principle of Evil; he alone has taken it upon himself to speak evil and exorcise it, he alone agrees to embody it in terror.

What lies behind his decision is beyond our understanding, and there is little to be gained from rambling on about the internal divisions within Islam. What we can state with certainty, however, is the superiority this affords him over the West, where the possibility of speaking evil no longer exists anywhere, where the slightest criticism, the slightest radical negativity is stifled by the virtual consensus on all values based on negotiation and reconciliation. Political power in the West now only half-heartedly exercises its former functions, one of which was to designate the Other, the Enemy, the stakes, the threat, the evil. Power exists only as long as it has this symbolic potency. It no longer has that potency today and, conversely, there is no opposition which is able or willing to designate the current powers-that-be as the evil. We are now very low on satanic, ironic, polemical, antagonistic energy; we have become fanatically soft societies, or softly fanatical ones.

By hounding out the 'accursed share' from within ourselves, and allowing only positive values to shine forth, we have become dramatically vulnerable to the slightest viral attack, including that of the Ayatollah, whose immune defences are certainly not down. The only thing we can range against him – and it is not much – is human rights, which is itself part of our political immunodeficiency. And, moreover, in the name of human rights, we end up describing the Ayatollah himself as 'absolute Evil' (Mitterand), that is to say, end up identifying with his irrational curse in a way that stands in total contradiction to our enlightened discourse (do we call a madman 'mad' today? We don't even call a handicapped person 'handicapped', so afraid are we of Evil, so much do we wallow in euphemisms in order to avoid designating the Other, misfortune, the irreducible).

We should not be surprised that someone capable of speaking the language of Evil – speaking it literally and triumphantly – should trigger such an access of weakness in Western cultures, in spite of petitions by intellectuals the world over. The fact is that legality, humanitarian good conscience and reason itself yield in the face of imprecation. Reason is completely fascinated by it and falls in with it, as do all the world's media. All it can do is mobilize its reserves of stigmatization and satanization, but, in so doing, it lapses into the same language and falls into the trap of the principle of Evil, which is essentially contagious. Who is the winner? The Ayatollah of course. Admittedly, we still have the power to destroy him, but symbolically he has won and symbolic power is always superior to the power of weapons and money; our modern idealism should have taught us that. It is, in a way, the revenge of the other world. The Third World had never really managed to mount a challenge to the West. And the USSR, which for a few decades personified the principle of Evil for the West, has clearly moved over quietly to the side of Good, the side of a well-tempered management of the world's affairs. By a marvellous irony, that country even offered itself as mediator between the West and the Satan of Teheran. And it has the experience to do that, having spent five years defending Western values in Afghanistan, without anyone properly realizing it. Some commentators have at least acknowledged, with some bitterness, that Khomeini's sentence has, by force of anathema, restored a fantastic value to books – a value they had lost. This is to recognize the shameful state politics has fallen into in our countries.

The effect of fascination, attraction and repulsion on a world scale, unleashed by the Ayatollah's death sentence on Rushdie, is exactly like the phenomenon of sudden depressurization of an aircraft cabin when there is a hole or crack in the fuselage (even if this is accidental, it always resembles a terrorist act). Everything is sucked violently outwards into the void, as a result of the pressure differential between the two spaces. You have only to make a breach, a hole in the ultra-thin film separating the two worlds. Terrorism, hostage-taking, is pre-eminently the act which makes this kind of breach in an artificial – and artificially protected – universe (our universe). The whole of Islam, *current* Islam, which is not in any sense the Islam of the Middle Ages, and which has to be assessed in strategic, not moral or religious terms, is creating a vacuum around the Western system (including the countries of Eastern Europe) and, from time to time, making breaches in that system, by a single act or statement, through which all our values hurtle out into the void. Islam does not exert revolutionary pressure on the Western world; there is no danger that Islam will convert or conquer it: it is happy to destabilize it by this viral aggression in the name of the principle of Evil (to which we have no answer) and on the basis of the virtual catastrophe that is the pressure differential between the two milieus – the perpetual risk for the protected universe (our universe) of a sudden de-pressurizing of the air (the values) we breathe. Admittedly, quite a bit of oxygen has already escaped from our Western world through all kinds of fissures and cracks. We would be well advised to hold on to our oxygen masks.

Our entire system rushes to serve the Ayatollah. He has merely to raise his little finger and the principle of Evil draws us to him in frenzied fascination. Contrary to all that is said of it, his strategy is astonishingly modern. Much more modern than ours, since it consists in subtly injecting archaic elements into a modern context: a *fatwa*, a decree of execution, a curse or any old thing. If our Western world were robust, this would simply be meaningless. But the whole of our system falls into the trap and becomes a sounding-box for these elements, a superconductor for the virus. How can we explain this? Once again, what we have here is the revenge of the Other World: we, in our time, infected the rest of the world with enough germs, diseases, epidemics and ideologies against which they had no resistance. Today, in an ironic twist, it seems we are ourselves defenceless in the face of a tiny little archaic microbe.

The hostage himself is becoming microbial. Alain Bosquet shows in his latest book (*Le Métier d'otage*) how, once deflected into the void, the hostage – that particle of the Western world – cannot go home, no longer wants to go home. For one thing he is demeaned in his own eyes, but also his own people, his country and fellow citizens are collectively demeaned by their enforced passivity, their routine cowardice, the very act of negotiation, which is degrading in itself and fundamentally useless. For, quite apart from the negotiation, every hostage-taking proves the inescapable cowardice of entire communities *vis-à-vis* the least significant of their members. And indeed, the indifference of the community to its members has its counterpart in the indifference of each individual to the community: this is how we function (badly) in the West and it is this political impoverishment which the strategy of hostage-taking ruthlessly exposes. By destabilizing a single individual, an entire system is destabilized. This is why the hostage cannot even forgive his own people for having made him into a hero – an elevation which in fact it immediately retracts.

We can neither get into the mind of the Ayatollah, nor into the hearts of Muslims, and there can be no question of espousing their passions or beliefs. All we can do is get away from that feeble, dogmatic thinking which imputes all this to religious fanaticism, and garner at least a glimmer of strategic understanding of what is at stake in this symbolic challenge; in this respect, the hotchpotch of pious and pathetic reactions one reads is next to useless and represents little but an attempt at exorcism.

I fear we are ill-equipped to meet the challenge of this symbolic violence of Islam at the very moment when we are trying to wipe the Terror from our memory of the revolution for the sake of a commemoration which, like the current consensus, has all the features of an inflatable structure. How are we to react to this new violence if we choose to blot out the violence of our own history?

14 March 1989

The Defrosting of Eastern Europe
and the End of History

The event of the end of the century is under way. The idea that history, stifled for a time by the grip of totalitarian ideology, is resuming its course with renewed vigour now that the blockade of the countries of Eastern Europe has been lifted, has put air back in everyone's lungs. The field of history is at last opened up again to the unpredictable movement of peoples and their thirst for freedom. In contrast to the depressive mythology which generally accompanies the ends of centuries, it seems this one is to usher in a new and illustrious resurgence of the final process, to bring fresh hope and a revival of all historical challenges. Away with all those evil auguries of the end of history. How can its reality and vitality be doubted when such events are taking place before our eyes?

Seen at closer quarters, the event is a bit more mysterious, and might with much greater accuracy be described as an unidentified 'historical' object. This thawing of the Eastern bloc, this thawing of liberty is certainly an extraordinary turn of events. But what becomes of liberty when it is defrosted? The operation is a perilous one and its outcome uncertain (even leaving aside the fact that what has been defrosted cannot be deep-frozen again). The USSR and the Eastern bloc have not just served as a deep-freeze for freedom; they have also provided a testing ground, an experimental environment in which it was sequestered and subjected to very high pressures. The West, for its part, is little more than a repository or, more accurately, a dumping ground for freedom and human rights. If ultra-freezing was the distinctive – and negative – mark of the Eastern world, the ultra-fluidity of our Western world is even more shocking since, as a consequence of the liberation and liberalization of mores and opinions, the problem of liberty quite simply cannot be posed here any longer. It is resolved virtually. In the West, freedom – the Idea of Freedom – has died a natural death: this we have seen in all the recent commemorations. In the East it was murdered, but there is no such thing as the perfect crime. It will be very interesting, from an experimental point of view, to see what freedom is like when it resurfaces, when it is resuscitated after all signs of it have been blotted out. We shall see what a process of reanimation or *post mortem* rehabilitation looks like. Perhaps defrosted liberty is not so attractive as all that. And what if it turned out to be intent on just one thing: bartering itself off in a binge of cars and electrical goods, not to mention mind-bending drugs and pornography; that is, immediately trading itself off against Western liquid assets, switching over from an end of history by deep-freezing to an end of history by ultra-fluidity and circulation?

The enthralling thing about these events in Eastern Europe is not to see them meekly coming to the aid of an ailing democracy by bringing it fresh energy (and new markets), but to see the telescoping of two specific patterns of the end of history: the one where it ends deep-frozen in the concentration camps and the other where, by contrast, it ends in the total, centrifugal expansion of communication. In each case, a final solution. And it may be that the unfreezing of human rights is the socialist equivalent of the 'depressurization of the West': a mere discharge into the Western void of the energies trapped for half a century in the East.

The fervour surrounding events can be deceptive: if that of the Eastern bloc countries is merely an ardent desire to be free of ideology, merely a fervent desire to imitate the free-market countries, where all liberty has already been exchanged for technological ease of living, then we shall see once and for all what freedom is worth and know that it can perhaps never be regained. History serves up no second helpings. On the other hand – and this is the unpredictable part for us, for the West (after all, when the Evil Empire collapses Good cannot remain exactly as it was before!) – this defrosting of the East may be as harmful in the long term as the surfeit of carbon gases in the upper layers of the atmosphere, creating a political greenhouse effect and such a warming of human relations on the planet, with the melting of the Communist ice-floes, that the shores of the West will be flooded. Curiously, whereas we dread the climatic melting of ice-floes and see it as representing a potential catastrophe, we long with all our might as democrats for such a thaw on the political front.

If, in the old days, the USSR had dumped its stock of gold on the world market, that market would have been completely destabilized. If the Eastern bloc countries were to put back into circulation the vast stock of freedom they have been keeping on ice, they would similarly destabilize the very fragile metabolism of Western values, which requires that freedom no longer manifest itself as action but as a virtual and consensual form of interaction, not as drama, but as the universal psychodrama of liberalism. A sudden injection of freedom as a lived relationship – as violent and active transcendence, as Idea – would be catastrophic in every way for our air-conditioned redistribution of values. Yet this is what we are asking of those in the East: the idea of freedom in exchange for the material signs of freedom. A perfectly diabolical pact, in which one side is in danger of losing its soul, the other its comfort.

But it is perhaps better this way. On both sides. The masked societies (the Communist societies) are now unmasked. What face do they present? It is a long time since we shed our masks, a long time since we had either masks or faces. We have no memory either. We have reached the point of seeking in water a memory without traces, of hoping (I crave Benveniste's indulgence here)[5] that something still remains when even the molecular traces have disappeared. It is the same with our freedom: we would be hard-pressed to produce any sign of it and we have reached the point of postulating its infinitesimal, impalpable, undetectable existence in a milieu of such high (programmatic, operational) dilution that only its spectre still hovers in a memory which is now merely the memory of water.

The wellspring of freedom has run so dry in the West (as witness the commemoration of the French Revolution) that we must place all our hopes in the East European deposits that have at last been uncovered and opened up. But once this stock of liberty has been released (the Idea of Liberty having become as scarce as a natural resource), what can ensue but, as on any market, an intense, superficial burst of trading, followed by a rapid collapse of differential energies and asset values.

What is the meaning of *glasnost*? The retrospective transparency of all the signs of modernity, speeded up and second-hand (it is almost a postmodern re-make of our original version of modernity) – of all the positive and negative signs combined: that is, not just human rights, but crimes, catastrophes and accidents which are, it seems, all joyously increasing in the former USSR since the liberalization of the regime. And even the rediscovery of pornography and extra-terrestrials, all previously censored, but celebrating their reappearance along with everything else. This is the experimental dimension of this general defrosting: we can now see that crimes and catastrophes, both nuclear and natural, along with everything else that

5. The 'memory of water affair' was the name generally applied in the media to Jacques Benveniste's claim in 1984 that he had discovered reactions produced by solutions so highly diluted that they 'contained only water molecules'.

has been repressed, are part of our human rights (the religious sphere too, of course, and fashion; indeed, nothing is debarred) – and this is a fine object lesson in democracy. For we see re-emerging here, in a kind of ideal hallucination and return of the repressed, all that we are, all the allegedly universal emblems of the human, including the worst, dullest, corniest things in Western 'culture' – things which will henceforth know no boundaries. It is, then, a moment of truth for that culture, as was the earlier confrontation with the primitive cultures of the whole world, a confrontation from which our culture cannot really be said to have emerged with flying colours. The irony of the situation is such that it will perhaps be we who are one day forced to rescue the historical memory of Stalinism, while the countries of Eastern Europe will no longer recall it. It will be up to us to keep on ice the memory of this tyrant who, for his part, kept the movement of history frozen, since that glacial age also forms part of our universal heritage.

These events are remarkable from another point of view too. They force us to enquire into the turn history is now taking; not simply proceeding towards its end (a notion that was part of the linear phantasm of history), but moving into reverse and into systematic obliteration. We are in the process of wiping out the entire twentieth century, effacing all the signs of the Cold War one by one, perhaps even all trace of the Second World War and of all the political or ideological revolutions of the twentieth century. The reunification of Germany is inevitable, as are many other things, not in the sense of a leap forward in history, but in the sense of a re-writing in reverse of the whole of the twentieth century, a re-writing which is going to take up a large part of the last ten years of the century. At the rate we are going we shall soon be back at the Holy Roman Empire. And perhaps this is the illumination this *fin de siècle* offers and the true meaning of that controversial formula, 'the end of history'. The fact is that, in a sort of enthusiastic work of mourning, we are in the process of retracting all the significant events of this century, of *whitewashing* the century, as if everything that had taken place (revolutions, the division of the world, exterminations, the violent transnationality of states, going to the nuclear brink – in short, history in its modern phase) were merely a hopeless imbroglio, and everyone had set about unmasking that history with the same enthusiasm that had gone into making it. Restoration, regression, rehabilitation, revival of the old frontiers, of the old differences, of particularities, of religions, resipiscence, even at the level of morals. It seems that all the signs of liberations achieved over a century are fading and will, in the end, perhaps be snuffed out one by one: we are into a gigantic process of *revisionism* – not an ideological revisionism but a revisionism of history itself, and we seem in a hurry to get it over before the end of the century, secretly hoping perhaps to be able to start again from scratch in the new millennium. If only we could restore everything to its initial state. But which initial state? Before the twentieth century? Before the Revolution? How far can this retraction, this restoration go? The fact is that it can move very, very quickly (as the events in Eastern Europe show), precisely because it is not a work of construction but a massive deconstruction of history, and one assuming almost viral, epidemic form. Perhaps even, in the end, the year 2000 will not take place, quite simply because the curve of history will have bent so far backwards that it will never cross that time horizon.

15 December 1989

No Pity for Sarajevo

In the TV programme *Le Couloir pour la parole* (broadcast on the 'Arte' channel, 19 December), with its Strasbourg–Sarajevo video link-up, the striking feature was the absolute superiority, the exceptional status conferred by misfortune, distress and total disillusionment – that very disillusionment which allowed the people of Sarajevo to treat the 'Europeans' with contempt, or at least with an air of sarcastic freedom, which contrasted with the hypocritical remorse and contrition of those at the other end of the video-link. It was not *they* who needed compassion; they had compassion for *our* wretched destinies. 'I spit on Europe', said one of them. Nothing offers greater freedom, in fact, or greater sovereignty, than justified contempt – and not even for the enemy, but for those sunning their good consciences in the warm glow of solidarity.

And they have seen plenty of these fine friends. Recently, even Susan Sontag, who came to stage *Waiting for Godot* in Sarajevo. Why not *Bouvard and Pécuchet* in Somalia or Afghanistan?[6] Yet the worst part of this isn't the high-flown cultural sentiment, but

6. *Bouvard et Pécuchet* was Flaubert's last, unfinished novel. It was published in serial form in the *Nouvelle Revue*, beginning on 15 December 1880, some seven months after his death.

the condescending attitude and the misconception regarding where strength and weakness lie. *They* are the strong ones. It is *we* who are weak, going over there searching for something to compensate for our weakness and loss of reality.

Our reality: that is the problem. We have only one reality, and it has to be rescued. And rescued even with the worst of slogans: 'We have to do something. We can't just do nothing'. But doing something just because you cannot not do it has never amounted to a principle of action or freedom. Merely a form of absolution from your own impotence and compassion for your own fate.

The people of Sarajevo do not have to face this question. Where they are, there is an absolute need to do what they do, to do what has to be done. With no illusions as to ends and no compassion for themselves. That is what being real means; that is what it means to be in the real. And this is not in any sense the 'objective' reality of their misfortune, that reality which *ought not to exist* and for which we feel pity, but the reality which exists as it is – the reality of an action and a destiny.

This is why they are alive and we are the ones who are dead. This is why, from our own point of view, we have, first, to rescue the reality of the war and impose that – compassionate – reality on those who are suffering from it, but who, at the very heart of war and distress, do not really believe in it.

In her opinion pieces, Susan Sontag confesses that the Bosnians do not really believe in the distress all around them. In the end, they find the whole situation unreal, senseless, unintelligible. It is a hell, but an almost hyperreal hell, made the more hyperreal by media and humanitarian harassment, since that makes the attitude of the whole world towards them even more incomprehensible. So, they live in a kind of spectral war – and a good thing too or they could never bear it. It is not I who say this; they say it themselves.

But Susan Sontag, who is from New York, must know better than they do what reality is because she has chosen them to embody it. Or perhaps simply because it is what she – and the whole of the West – lacks most. So it is necessary to go and rebuild a reality for ourselves where the bleeding is. All these 'corridors' we open up to send our supplies and our 'culture' are, in reality, corridors of distress through which we import their strength and the energy generated by their misfortune. Once again, an unequal exchange. And Susan Sontag comes to convince them – they who find a kind of additional strength in the thorough stripping-away of the illusion of the real (including the principle of political rationality by which we are governed, and which is part of the European reality principle) – of the 'reality' of their suffering, by culturalizing it, of course, by theatricalizing it so that it can serve as a point of reference in the theatre of Western values, one of which is solidarity.

Yet Susan Sontag herself is not the issue. She is merely fashionably emblematic of what has now become a widespread situation, in which harmless, powerless intellectuals trade their woes with the wretched, each supporting the other in a kind of perverse contract – exactly as the political class and civil society trade their respective woes today, the one serving up its corruption and scandals, the other its artificial convulsions and inertia. Not so long ago, we saw Bourdieu and the Abbé Pierre offering themselves up in televisual sacrifice, trading off between them the pathos-laden language and the sociological meta-language of misery.[7] And so, also, our entire society is embarked on the path of commiseration in the literal sense, under cover of ecumenical pathos. It is almost as though, in a moment of intense repentance among intellectuals and politicians, a moment related to the panic currently surrounding history and the twilight of values, we had to replenish the stocks of values, the referential reserves, by appealing to that lowest common

---

7. The Abbé Pierre has been a prominent French figure since the 1950s, being particularly well known for his work with the homeless. Pierre Bourdieu was Professor of Sociology at the Collège de France and Director of Studies at the École des Hautes Études en Sciences Sociales.

denominator that is human misery, restocking the hunting grounds with artificial game, as it were. 'It is currently impossible, in news and documentaries, to show any other spectacle than suffering' (Daniel Schneidermann). A victim society. I suppose all it is doing is expressing its own disappointment and remorse for an unthinkable violence against itself.

The New Intellectual Order everywhere treads the paths marked out by the New World Order. The misfortune, suffering and misery of others have everywhere become the raw material and the primal scene. Victimhood, accompanied by human rights, as the only, funereal, ideology. Those who do not exploit it directly and in their own name do so by proxy. And there is no lack of middlemen who take their financial or symbolic cut in the process. Deficit and misfortune, like the international debt, are traded and sold on in the futures market – in this case the politico-intellectual market, which is quite the equal of the late, unlamented military–industrial complex.

Now, all commiseration is part of the logic of misfortune. To refer to misfortune, if only to combat it, is to give it a base for objective reproduction in perpetuity. When fighting against anything whatever, we have to start out from the evil to be combated, never from the misfortune produced.

And the theatre of the transparency of Evil is truly there – in Sarajevo. The suppressed canker which corrupts all the rest, the virus of which Europe's paralysis is the symptom. Europe's irons are being pulled out of the fire at the GATT talks, but things are going up in smoke at Sarajevo. In a sense, this is a good thing. The specious, sham Europe, the Europe botched together in the most hypocritical convulsions, is coming unstuck at Sarajevo. And in this sense we might almost see the Serbs as providing the unofficial acid test, as demystifying that phantom Europe – the Europe of technocratic politicians who are as triumphalist in their speeches as they are deliquescent in their actions. For we can see that the more talk there is of Europe, the more it decays (just as the more talk there is of human rights, the less they are respected). But this is not the real point here. The real story is that the Serbs, as the agents of ethnic cleansing, are at the forefront of the construction of Europe. For it *is* being constructed, the 'real' Europe: a white Europe, a white-washed Europe, integrated and purified morally as much as economically or ethnically. It is being victoriously constructed at Sarajevo and, in this sense, what is happening there is not an accident at all, but a logical, ascendant phase in the New European Order, that subsidiary of the New World Order, everywhere character-ized by 'white' fundamentalism, protectionism, discrimination and control.

It is said that if we just leave things to happen at Sarajevo we shall be the next to 'get it'. But we have already got it. All the European countries are undergoing ethnic cleansing. This is the real Europe taking shape in the shadow of the Parliaments, and its spearhead is Serbia. It is no use talking about some sort of pas-sivity or powerlessness to react, since what we have here is a programme currently being carried out, a programme in which Bosnia is merely the new frontier. Why do you think Le Pen has largely disappeared from the political stage? Because the substance of his ideas has everywhere filtered into the political class in the form of national opt-outs, cross-party unity, Euro-nationalist instincts and protectionism. There is no need now for Le Pen, since he has won, not politically, but virally – in mentalities. Why should this stop at Sarajevo, since what is at stake is exactly the same? Solidarity will not make a jot of difference to all this. It will end miraculously the day the extermination is complete, the day the demarcation line of 'white' Europe has been drawn. It is as though Europe, irrespective of national distinctions and political differences, had 'taken out a contract' with the Serbs, who have done the dirty deed for it, as the West once took out a contract on Iran with Saddam Hussein. Only, when the hired gun goes too far, he too may have to be bumped off. The operations against Iraq and Somalia were relative failures from the point of view of the New World Order; so far as the New European Order is concerned, the Bosnian operation seems set to succeed.

The Bosnians know this. They know they are condemned by the international democratic order, not by some hangover from the past or some monstrous excrescence called fascism. They know they are doomed to be exterminated or banished or excluded, like all heterogeneous, refractory elements the world over – irrevocably so because, whether the kind souls and bad consciences of the West like it or not, that is the inexorable path of progress. The price to pay for modern Europe will be the eradication of Muslims and Arabs, who are indeed already being eradicated everywhere, except where they remain as immigrant slaves. And the major objection to the bad-conscience offensive, as mobilized in media happenings like the one at Strasbourg, is that, by perpetuating the image of the alleged powerlessness of European policies and the image of a Western conscience racked by its own impotence, it provides a cover for the real operation by lending it the spiritual benefit of the doubt.

The people of Sarajevo shown on Arte certainly looked as if they had no illusions and no hope, but they did not look like potential martyrs. Far from it. They had their objective misfortune, but the real wretchedness, that of the false apostles and voluntary martyrs, was on the other side. Now, as has very rightly been said, 'in the hereafter no heed will be paid to voluntary martyrdom'.

7 January 1993

Otherness Surgery

With modernity, we enter the age of the production of the Other. The aim is no longer to kill the Other, devour it, seduce it, vie with it, love it or hate it, but, in the first instance, to produce it. The Other is no longer an object of passion, but an object of production. Perhaps, in its radical otherness or its irreducible singularity, the Other has become dangerous or unbearable, and its seductive power has to be exorcized? Or perhaps, quite simply, otherness and the dual relation progressively disappear with the rise of individual values and the destruction of symbolic ones? The fact remains that otherness does come to be in short supply and, *if we are not to live otherness as destiny, the other has to be produced imperatively as difference.* This goes for the world as much as for the body, sex and social relations. It is to escape the world as destiny, the body as destiny, sex (and the opposite sex) as destiny, that the production of the other as difference will be invented. For example, sexual difference: each sex with its anatomical and psychological characteristics, with its own desire and all the irresolvable consequences that ensue, including the ideology of sex and the utopia of a difference based both in right and in nature. None of this has any meaning in seduction, where it is a question not of desire but of a game with desire, and where it is a question not of the equality of the sexes or the alienation of the one by the other, since game-playing involves a perfect reciprocity of part-ners (not difference and alienation, but otherness and complicity). Seduction is as far from hysteria as can be. Neither of the sexes projects its sexuality on to the other; the distances are given; otherness is intact – it is the very condition of that higher illusion that is play with desire.

However, with the coming of the nineteenth century and Romanticism, a *mas-culine hysteria* comes into play and with it a change in the sexual paradigm, which we must once again situate within the more general, universal framework of the change in the paradigm of otherness.

In this hysterical phase, it was, so to speak, the femininity of man which pro-jected itself on to woman and shaped her as an ideal figure in his image. In Romantic love, the aim was not now to conquer the woman, to seduce her, but to create her from the inside, to invent her, in some cases as achieved utopian vision, as idealized woman, in others as *femme fatale*, as star – another hysterical, supernat-ural metaphor. The Romantic Eros can be credited with having invented this ideal of harmony, of loving fusion, this ideal of an almost incestuous form of twin beings – the woman as projective resurrection of the same, who assumes her super-natural form only as ideal of the same, an artefact doomed henceforth to *l'amour* or, in other words, to a pathos of the ideal resemblance of beings and sexes – a pathetic confusion which substitutes for the dual otherness of seduction. The whole mechanics of the erotic changes meaning, for the erotic attraction which previously arose out of otherness, out of the strangeness of the Other, now finds its stimulus in sameness – in similarity and resemblance. Auto-eroticism, incest? No. Rather a hypostasis of the Same. Of the same eyeing up the other, investing itself in the other, alienating itself in the other – but the other is only ever the ephemeral form of a difference which brings me closer to me. This indeed is why, with Romantic love and all its current spin-offs, sexuality becomes connected with death: it is because it becomes connected with incest and its destiny – even in banalized form (for we are no longer speaking of mythic, tragic incest here; with modern eroticism we are dealing with a secondary incestuous form – of the protection of the same in the image of the other – which amounts to a confusion and corruption of all images).

We have here then, in the end, the invention of a femininity which renders woman superfluous. The invention of a difference which is merely a roundabout copulation with its double. And which, at bottom, renders any encounter with otherness impossible (it would be interesting to know whether there was not any hysterical quid pro quo from the feminine in the construction of a virile, phallic mythology; feminism being one such example of the hystericization of the masculine in woman, of the hysterical projection of her masculinity in the exact image of the hysterical projection by man of his femininity into a mythical image of woman).

However, there still remains a dissymmetry in this enforced assignment to difference.

This is why I have contended, paradoxically, that man is more different from woman than woman is from man. I mean that, within the framework of sexual difference, man is merely different, whereas in woman there remains something of the radical otherness which precedes the debased status of difference.

In short, in this process of extrapolation of the Same into the production of the Other, of hysterical invention of the sexual other as twin sister or brother (if the twin theme is so prominent today, that is because it reflects this mode of libidinal cloning), the sexes become progressively assimilated to each other. This develops from difference to lesser difference through to the point of role-reversal and the virtual non-differentiation of the sexes. And it ends up making sexuality a useless function. In cloning, for example, pointlessly sexed beings are going to be reproduced, since sexuality is no longer needed for their reproduction.

If the real woman seems to disappear in this hysterical invention of the feminine (though she has other means of resisting this), in this invention of sexual difference, in which the masculine occupies the privileged pole from the outset, and in which all the feminist struggles will merely reassert that insoluble privilege or difference, we must recognize too that masculine desire also becomes entirely problematical since it is able only to project itself into another in its image and, in this way, render itself purely speculative. So all the nonsense about the phallus and male sexual privilege, etc. needs revising. There is a kind of transcendent justice which means that, in this process of sexual differentiation which culminates inexorably in non-differentiation, the two sexes each lose as much of their singularity and their otherness. This is the era of the Transsexual, in which all the conflicts connected with this sexual difference carry on long after any real sexuality, any real alterity of the sexes, has disappeared.

Each individual repeats on his or her own body this (successful?) takeover of the feminine by masculine projection hysteria. The body is identified and appropriated as a self-projection, and no longer as otherness and destiny. In the facial features, in sex, in sickness and death, identity is constantly being altered. You can do nothing about that. It is destiny. But this is precisely what has to be warded off at all costs in the identification of the body, the individual appropriation of the body, of your desire, your appearance, your image: plastic surgery on all fronts. For if the body is no longer a site of otherness, of a dual relation, if it is a site of identification, then you have urgently to reconcile yourself with it, to repair it, perfect it, turn it into an ideal object. Everyone treats his/her body as man treats woman in the projective identification we have described: he invests it as a fetish in a desperate attempt at self-identification. The body becomes an object of autistic worship, of an almost incestuous manipulation. And it is the body's resemblance to its model which becomes a source of eroticism and unconsummated self-seduction, insofar as it virtually excludes the Other and is the best means of excluding any seduction from elsewhere.

Many other things relate also to this production of the Other – a hysterical, speculative production. Racism is one example, in its development throughout the modern era and its current recrudescence. Logically, it ought to have declined with progress and the spread of Enlightenment. But the more we learn how unfounded the genetic theory of race is, the more racism intensifies. This is because we are dealing with an artificial construction of the Other, on the basis of an erosion of the singularity of cultures (of their otherness one to another) and entry into the fetishistic system of difference. So long as there is otherness, alienness and a (possibly violent) dual relation, there is no racism properly so called. That is to say, roughly, up to the eighteenth century, as anthropological accounts attest. Once this 'natural' relation is lost, we enter upon an exponential relation with an artificial Other. And there is nothing in our culture with which we can stamp out racism, since the entire movement of that culture is towards a fanatical differential construction of the Other, and a perpetual extrapolation of the Same through the Other. Autistic culture posing as altruism.

We talk of alienation. But the worst alienation is not being dispossessed *by* the other, but being dispossessed *of* the other: it is having to produce the other in the absence of the other, and so continually to be thrown back on oneself and one's own image. If, today, we are condemned to our image (to cultivate our bodies, our 'looks', our identities, our desires), this is not because of alienation, but because of the end of alienation and the virtual disappearance of the other, which is a much worse fate. In fact, the definition of alienation is to take oneself as one's focus, as one's object of care, desire, suffering and communication. This definitive short-circuiting of the other ushers in the era of transparency. Plastic surgery becomes universal. And the surgery performed on the face and the body is merely the symptom of a more radical surgery: that performed on otherness and destiny.

What is the solution? There is no solution to this erotic trend within an entire culture; to this fascination, this whirl of denial of otherness, of all that is alien and negative; to this foreclosing of evil and this reconciliation around the Same and its multiple figures: incest, autism, twinship, cloning. All we can do is remind ourselves that seduction lies in non-reconciliation with the other, in preserving the alien status of the Other. One must not be reconciled with oneself or with one's body. One must not be reconciled with the other, one must not be reconciled with nature, one must not be reconciled with the feminine (that goes for women too). Therein lies the secret of a strange attraction.

5 July 1993

The Powerlessness of the Virtual

A recent episode: students demonstrate and hold up the TGV in Angoulême station. They pour down both sides of the train, past the passengers sitting motionless behind their tinted windows. A shout here and a slogan there. An occasional outburst of rage – but against whom? It is as though they were barking at an artificial satellite. For the TGV is virtual reality crossing France *in vitro* – an embodiment of speed, money and all those things which circulate – confronted here with *their* very real world of potential unemployment. A surrealistic confrontation between time's arrow and a youth already spent. All they will wrest from the transparency of the rich is this ten minutes of immobility, this ten-minute freezing of the TV spectacle of which they are the victims.

A scaled-down version of the clash between the real and the virtual and its fantastic consequences at the planetary level: the dissociation between a very high-frequency virtual space and a zero-frequency real space. The two no longer have anything in common, nor is there any communication between them: the unconditional extension of the virtual (which includes not just the new images or remote simulation, but the whole cyberspace of geo-finance, the space of multimedia and the information superhighways) brings with it an unprecedented desertification of real space and of all that surrounds us. The information superhighways will have the same effect as our present superhighways or motorways. They will cancel out the landscape, lay waste to the territory and abolish real distances. What is merely physical and geographical in the case of our motorways will assume its full dimensions in the electronic field with the abolition of mental distances and the absolute shrinkage of time. All short circuits (and the establishment of this planetary hyperspace is tantamount to one immense short circuit) produce electric shocks. What we see emerging here is no longer merely territorial desert, but social desert, employment desert, the body itself being laid waste by the very concentration of information. A kind of Big Crunch, contemporaneous with the Big Bang of the financial markets and the information networks. We are merely at the dawning of the process, but the waste and the wastelands are already growing much faster than the computerization process itself. The two worlds, though literally cut off from each other, are equally exponential. But the discrepancy between them does not create any new political situation or genuine crisis, for memory fades at the same time as does the real. The discrepancy is only virtually catastrophic.

Another catastrophic prospect, of which none of the champions of the virtual of whatever stamp have any inkling (whether we are talking of the occult masters of world finance or the proponents of a universal democracy of information), is the phenomenon of *critical mass*. We know how this operates at the cosmological level: if the mass of the universe is below a certain threshold, the universe goes on expanding and the Big Bang goes on to infinity. If it is above this threshold, the universe implodes and contracts in a Big Crunch. Now, without wishing to exaggerate, the sphere of information (understanding by this, once again, the orbital circulation in real time both of money and images or messages) is in danger, given the prospect of infinite development – the universal connection of all the networks we are promised – of experiencing a brutal reversion of the same kind. With the information superhighways, it would seem we are doing all we can to get beyond this critical threshold. Where its dewy-eyed advocates see only a marvellous centrifugal expansion, are we not moving towards such a degree of saturation and density that a deflation and automatic collapse will ensue? And this eventuality is no longer the product of a discrepancy between an ultra-sophisticated, ultra-connected sphere and the wasteland of the rest of the world (the information Fourth World), but a catastrophe internal to the virtual high-tech world – an implosion by exceeding of the critical mass.

We may indeed ask ourselves whether we have not already passed this threshold and whether the information catastrophe has not already occurred, insofar as the multimedia profusion of data cancels itself out and the balance sheet in terms of substance of information is already a negative one. There is a precedent here in the form of the 'social': we are already well beyond the threshold of the critical social mass with the profusion of populations, control networks, socialization, communication, interactivity and with the extrapolation of the 'social' as a catch-all category – a move which is even now causing the real sphere of the social and its concept to implode. When everything is social, suddenly nothing is.

But perhaps beneath this crazed technological optimism, this messianic incantation of the virtual, our dream is of just this critical threshold, and this phase-reversal of the sphere of information. Not having experienced this momentous event, this general implosion at the world level, we might be said to be enjoying it experimentally, at the level of a micro-model. Given the acceleration of the process, it may not be far from actually occurring. We should, then, heartily encourage this massive meltdown of information and communication.

At any rate, there is still an alternative hypothesis. This is that the picture we are given of the power of virtual technologies – from the irresistible promotion of virtual reality to the uncontrollable power of those new masters of the universe, the lords of Microsoft and tele-capitalism (*Le Monde diplomatique*, May 1995) – largely represents media hype reflecting the self-hyping of those milieus themselves (the whole process is a self-driving loop).

One of two things must be the case. Either the whole world is in thrall to these technological barons, who might be said to be concentrating every kind of real *power* in their own hands; in this case, all we can do is disappear, since in this scenario we are already virtually wiped off the map – and the territory. Or this is not the way things are at all and this whole story is virtual too. The power of the virtual is merely virtual. This is why it can intensify in such a mind-boggling way and, moving ever further from the so-called 'real' world, itself lose hold of any reality principle. For these technical forces to extend their grip over the world, they would have to have a purpose – power must be power to some *end* – but they do not. All they can do is transcribe themselves indefinitely into their own networks, their own codes. Even speculative capital rarely comes out of its orbit: it is amassed and lost in its own speculative vacuum. As for the transformation of this media power into political power, we have seen, in the case of Berlusconi, that it failed at the first hurdle, contrary to the thesis of the media *coup d'état* (according to which, once you had gained control of the economy and communications, it was merely a formality to seize political power).[8] We were frightened by an over-estimation of media power, whilst the media in fact sap the reality of all power, for better or for worse. It is an inevitable consequence of virtuality:

8. Berlusconi's government lasted for seven months, falling when Umberto Bossi's Lega Nord pulled out of the coalition.

there can be no strategy *of* the virtual, since the only strategies now are themselves virtual ones.

So there are no 'masters of the universe'. There are only masters of transparency, and just because their money, products and ideas cross the borders of a globalized market unhindered, that is no reason to bend the knee to this supremacy of the virtual in what would merely be a new form of voluntary servitude.

6 June 1995

Western Subserbience

It has taken a superhuman effort and three years of sporadic massacres, and, most importantly, it has needed the forces of the international community to be humiliated, but it seems that – grudgingly and with every possible reservation – Western opinion has finally recognized the Serbs as the aggressors. This recognition seems to represent the ultimate in firmness and lucidity. The fact is that we have, at last, got to the starting line in this war. Even those who reject the official doctrine of the 'belligerents' and are long-standing critics of Serb aggression are celebrating this turnabout as a victory, naively hoping that the Western powers now have no alternative but to put an end to the aggression. Clearly, nothing of the kind will occur. This entirely platonic recognition of the victimizers as victimizers in no way entails recognizing the victims as victims. To be fooled into thinking that it does, one has to share the evangelical idealism of those who believe that the 'depths of ridicule and dishonour' have been plumbed and that the international powers and a 'suicidal' Europe can be called on to recover themselves, without realizing for a moment the futility of such efforts. This, indeed, is every bit a match for the politicians' endless hypocrisy. Recrimination goes hand in glove with the crime, and the two proliferate in an interminable orchestration of the event. Since the Western conscience takes it upon itself to mourn the situation, since it monopolizes both the hypocrisy and good intentions, it is understandable that the murderer should retain his monopoly both of arrogance and crime.

In fact, neither the grotesque gesticulations of the international forces nor the disgusted lamentations of the representatives of good causes can have any real effect, because we have not taken the decisive step – the final step – in the analysis of the situation. No one dares, or wants, to take that step, which is to recognize, not simply that the Serbs are the aggressors (which is to state the obvious), but that they are our objective allies in a cleansing operation for a future Europe where there are no awkward minorities and for a New World Order where there is no radical opposition to its own values – the values of the democratic dictatorship of human rights and the transparency of markets.

In all this, it is the question of the evil which is at issue. Having denounced the Serbs as 'dangerous psychopaths', we congratulate ourselves on having pinpointed the evil without doubting for a second the purity of our democratic intentions. We believe we have done all that is needful by pointing to the Serbs as bad – but not as the enemy. And with good reason, since, on the world front, we Westerners and Europeans are fighting exactly the same enemy as they are: Islam, the Muslims. We are fighting them everywhere: in Chechnya with the Russians (where the West displays the same shameful tolerance); in Algeria, where we denounce the military government while providing all-out logistical support (there, as if by chance, the fine souls who stigmatize the official doctrine of the 'belligerents' in Bosnia use precisely the same language: state terrorism against fundamentalist terrorism – the one side as bad as the other. And we, the impotent onlookers amid this barbarism – as though state terrorism were not precisely our terrorism – already use it in our own countries in homeopathic doses). In short, we may well bombard a few Serb positions with smoke bombs, but we will not really intervene against them since they are doing basically the same work as we are. We would more readily break the backs of the victims if we had to, to settle the conflict. The victims, when they put up some token defence, are much more awkward than their persecutors and you will see that it will be the Bosnian Muslims the Rapid Intervention Force are soon forced to liquidate and neutralize. If a sizeable Muslim offensive were mounted, then you would see the international force becoming really effective.

This is the real reason why this war is interminable. If we think about it, without this deep-level collusion, despite all appearances (but the appearances, in their ambiguity, tell their own story), without this objective alliance (without it being intentional or deliberate), there is no reason why the war should not already be over. It is exactly the same scenario as with Saddam Hussein. We fought him with the full panoply of media and technological deployment. But he was nonetheless – and remains still – our objective ally. He has been reviled, denounced and stigmatized in the name of human rights, but he is nonetheless our objective ally against Iran, against the Kurds, against the Shi'ites. And that is one of the reasons why that war (the Gulf War) did not really take place: Saddam never was our real enemy. And it is the same with the Serbs, for whom in a way we provide cover, denouncing them as beyond the pale, while continuing to let them do their work.

The whole problem is to convince the Bosnians they are responsible for their own predicament. If we cannot do this by diplomacy, as we have been trying to do for two years, we shall have to do so by force. We should, all the same, attempt to see what is going on behind the enormous smokescreen, behind the stereotyped humanitarian, military and diplomatic language. In any conflict, you have to distinguish between what is being fought against – the specifically political level of the war – and what is being sacrificed – what, in particular, is being liquidated and swept away: this remains the thing most deeply at issue, the final objective. In the Algerian war, for example, we fought against the Algerian army, but what was really sacrificed in the conflict was the Algerian revolution – and this we did working alongside the Algerian army (and we continue to do so). In Bosnia we are fighting the Serbs (without overdoing it) in the name of a multicultural Europe, but what is actually being sacrificed is precisely the other culture, the culture which stands opposed at the level of values to an undifferentiated world order with no values. And this we are doing at the Serbs' side.

Imperialism has changed. What the West now wishes to foist on the whole world, in the guise of universality, is not its – completely unhinged – values, but its absence of values. Wherever some singularity, minority or specific idiom survives and persists; wherever there is some irreducible belief or passion; above all, where there is some antagonistic view of the world, we have to impose an in-different order upon it – an order as indifferent as we are to our own values. We generously distribute the right to difference, but secretly, and on this occasion unyieldingly, we are working to produce a bloodless, undifferentiated world.

This particular terrorism is not fundamentalist. Indeed, it is the terrorism of a culture without fundaments. It is the integrism of emptiness. What is at stake here is beyond political forms and events. We are no longer speaking of a political front or relation of forces, but of a transpolitical fault line, and that fault line today passes mainly through Islam. But it also runs through the heart of every so-called civilized, democratic country – and it certainly runs through every one of us.

3 July 1995

When the West Takes the Dead Man's Place[9]

Western military impotence in the face of Serbian aggression equates directly with the impossibility of risking the life of a single Western soldier. In this sense, these soldiers are hostages long before the Serbs actually capture them: their lives have to be preserved above all else. Zero death: this is the leitmotif of clean warfare. It is the perfection of war, but also war reduced to a mockery – war as faultless sporting performance, as 'clear round'. We have already seen this with the Gulf War, where the only Western deaths occurred by accident. At least that war ended in a technological demonstration which provided the illusion of power (of virtual omnipotence). Whereas Bosnia offers an example of total powerlessness. And though this powerlessness, which gives the Serbs a free rein, in fact fits in with the undisclosed objective of the war, it amounts, nonetheless, to a symbolic castration of the

9. *Quand l'Occident prend la place du mort*. The term 'la place du mort' owes its currency to the fact that it is used, in everyday parlance, to refer to the front passenger seat in a car. It is also occasionally employed as an image to represent the position of the analyst in the psychoanalytic relationship. Here, however, Baudrillard is using the term rather more literally.

Western war machine. The poor old West! If only it could joyfully and victoriously fulfil its mission of establishing world Order (by liquidating all the pockets of resistance), but it still has to look on impotently, from the depths of its riven conscience, while that dirty little job is carried out at the global level by mercenaries. To look on impotently while it is itself humiliated and sidelined.

There is, however, nothing surprising about this military paralysis. It is linked to the mental paralysis of the civilized world. We might think that the fact the West can no longer risk the life of a single one of its soldiers represents some higher stage of civilization, in which even the military has become committed to humanitarianism and respect for the sacred rights of human life. In fact, quite the opposite is the case. The destiny of this virtual soldier – this soldier who no longer is a soldier – reflects the destiny of civilized man. The things he fought for and his collective values have largely disappeared; his existence cannot be sacrificed for anything whatever. Only a thing which has some value in itself can be put 'at stake'.

The individual we have produced, the absolutely self-regarding individual we glorify, the individual we protect in his impotence with the whole legal panoply of human rights is the 'last man' Nietzsche speaks of. He is the end-user of his own self and his own life, the terminal individual, with no real hope either of descendants or transcendence. He is the end-of-the-line man, doomed to hereditary sterility and the countdown. This individual is the end of the cycle and of the species. All that remains for him is to attempt desperately to outlive himself by being spectralized, fractalized, pluralized, by becoming his own creation and his own clone. This last man cannot, then, be sacrificed, precisely because he is the last. Once life is reduced to its use-value, to its survival in real time, then no one has the right to risk his life for anything. This is the destiny – or, rather, the absence of destiny – of the last man. This is the way his impotence has developed, reflecting the development of the civilized nations, incapable even of taking the risk of facing up to their enemies – or saving face.

At a deep level the two things are connected: the elimination of any foreign culture, any singular minority in the name of ethnic cleansing, and the elimination of death itself as singularity, as irreducible fact – the most singular of singularities – in the name of protection and survival at all costs. Our lives are also being cleansed or purified in a sense. They are increasingly being played out inside a virtual carapace protecting them from death, in much the same way as the virtual soldier of the UN goes around in his technical carapace. Even when he is taken hostage, that doesn't make him any more real. He merely becomes a trading item in the potlatch of illusory divergences and collusions between the West and the Serbs, in the improbable chain of collusion and cowardice that is this military masquerade, in which the place of the unknown soldier is taken by the virtual soldier – the one who does not die, but who, paralysed and immobilized, takes the dead man's place. So we are seeing a redeployment of death in all these forms where we no longer expected to find it.

Take UNPROFOR and the Rapid Reaction Force: they too immediately took the dead man's place (which they defend tooth and nail!) in the Bosnian conflict. We ourselves, all of us behind our TV screens, are surreptitiously taking the place of the dead. The Serbs, the murderers, are alive in their own way. The people of Sarajevo, the victims, are in a place of real death. But we are in a strange situation: neither dead, nor alive, but standing in for the dead. And in this sense the Bosnian conflict is a global test; everywhere in the present world, the West has taken the place of the dead.

And yet this is not for want of trying to avert this situation by all available means. We almost pulled off the old trick of the Swiss who, for years, supplied the whole of Europe with mercenaries and thereby managed to keep free of wars. This is what all the rich countries do today – providing weapons for the whole world and succeeding in that way in exiling, if not violence, then at least war, from their territories. But there is nothing to be done; just where we hope to drive out death, it surfaces again through all the protective screens, extending to the furthest reaches of our culture.

Our humanitarian and ecological ideologies all speak to us of nothing but the human species and its survival. We can see here the great difference there is between humanitarianism and humanism. Humanism was a system of strong values linked to the concept of the human race, with its philosophy and morality. It was character-istic of a history that was being made. Whereas humanitarianism is a system of weak values, linked to the safeguarding of the threatened human species and character-istic of a history that is being unmade, that is coming apart; and there is no perspective here other than the negative one of an optimal management of waste – waste which we know to be, by definition, non-degradable. Seen in terms of survival or, in other words, of life superstitiously prolonged and protected from death, life itself becomes a waste-product we can no longer rid ourselves of, doomed, as it is, to indefinite reproduction.

Now, it is just such indefinite reproduction we see in Bosnia, just such a macabre parody and the sinister confusion of a history coming apart – a farce in which the military and the humanitarian are merged.

History reproducing itself becomes Farce.

Farce reproducing itself becomes History.

17 July 1995

The Great Laundering

Whitewashing is the main activity of this century's end. With the first three-quarters of the century largely given over to an accumulation of evils, violence, corruption and guilt, we have a colossal rubbish heap before us. We are engaged in an indefinite work of mourning for all the ideologies, violence and incidents which have marked the century. Repentance of the past, history being sold off at knock-down prices or given a face-lift. The whitewashing of a dirty history, of dirty money, of corrupt consciences, of the polluted planet.

The cleansing of memory; the cleansing of the environment; the ethnic and racial cleansing of populations. In particular, the political class has entered the victimal era of repentance. Every politician, everyone in a position of power, is potentially liable to prosecution and has to be laundered like dirty money. They have to submit, if not to a brainwashing, then at least to a reputation-washing, before being put back into circulation, the way blood is washed before it is reinjected into the body's circulation (this was not, in fact, done in the case of AIDS and it has given the political class its biggest scandal for years – the contaminated blood virus circulating even faster through the political system than through the systems of the patients).[10]

One has, where possible, to show off one's vices to restore one's virtue. This has even become a kind of fashionable political tactic: protesting one's errors, one's corruption, one's immorality; attempting at all costs to be found guilty. It is a kind of simulated expiation, a way of whitewashing oneself which the public conscience eagerly swallows at little cost to itself. Not everyone can whitewash themselves by committing suicide, as Pierre Bérégovoy did.[11] By that very act, he whitewashed the whole of the political class (by making politics a noble calling, since you can die by it), but this was also something of a poisoned chalice, as he simultaneously showed up the wretchedness and cowardice of all those who, though suffering the same powerlessness and dishonour – i.e. having the same reasons to do away with themselves – took considerable pains not to do so.

This same perspective of the whitewashing and face-lifting of the political class casts light also on the judiciary's anti-corruption offensive. That so-called 'Clean Hands' offensive makes the headlines daily, ranking alongside the lives of the stars. The situation is as follows: the political class was fretting away in its immunity and impunity. It was dying – weightless and far removed from the social body – on the far side of representation, in the tele-absence of the masses, in an immunity which had become lethal, while the tele-citizen, who had himself become auto-immune,

10. In spite of a circular of 1983 pointing out the risk, France continued to use blood from potentially contaminated sources in the 1980s, with the result that seven people contracted AIDS. Three ministers stood trial on manslaughter charges, but only one, Edmond Hervé, was convicted, though no sentence was passed on him.

11. Pierre Bérégovoy, the third prime minister of Mitterand's presidency, committed suicide on 1 May 1993, apparently because of damage done to his reputation by a scandal over an interest-free loan.

looked on. The media class had the same problem. It too was dying on the far side of the screen, in its tele-immunity. Hence the need for a huge 'reality show', an interactive perfusion, which could give the masses a role as fully-fledged extras. In the political field, the absolute imperative was also to remove this impunity by any means whatever – including being accused of wrongdoing, being exposed by scandal – so as to give the politicians the chance to overcome their isolation and reattach the umbilical cord.

For the political class, this was a matter of life and death. Now, that class is not capable of giving up its own privileges: it is capable only, as we have seen, of granting itself a general amnesty. In a sense, then, the politicians delegate this work to the judges. They use the judiciary to absolve them of their supposed immunity and isolation and overcome the public disaffection afflicting them. And they do this by appearing vulnerable and fragile, and hence open and accessible.

It is a great illusion to believe that, in our system, the politicians and the judiciary can really come into conflict. What is going on is merely a division of labour within a caste carrying out a simulated purge on itself – destabilizing itself in homeopathic doses the better to re-stabilize itself. There is, however, nothing to indicate that this stability has any long-term prospects. There is nothing to say the invoice for this laundering (after the laundering of the 'invoices')[12] – together with the bill for the collective brainwashing which accompanies it – will not one day land on the government's doorstep. The media and the political class will pay dearly. They are already paying for the loan they have taken out against our imaginary advance, by forfeiting all credence and credibility.

12. A series of scandals involving false invoices rocked France throughout the eighties and nineties, from the Urba affair, in which monies were laundered through a consultancy company into Socialist Party coffers, to the *affaires* associated with the names of Alain Carignon and Michel Noir.

There has recently been a widely orchestrated campaign against the presidential amnesty on grounds of public morality.[13] It is, in fact, the first time motorists have had such a secondary gain from elections to look forward to.

But perhaps this 'immoral' behaviour was compensation for the absence of any political stakes in these elections? At least in this way the citizens re-injected some real issues into them. At any rate, they expressed the truth of the elections themselves, which are no longer so much a political act of representation as a collective act – underwritten by a blank cheque from the people – of the obliteration and absolution of all corruption, all previous political wretchedness. Scandals, failures, embezzlement and simple mistakes are all whitewashed and amnestied for a moment. The Right has won, the Left is reborn from its ashes – everything starts off again from scratch. This is the marvellous illusionism of the electoral system! So we're not talking about an amnesty for petty lawbreaking here, but a general amnesty of the political system as a whole (the anything but petty larceny of the financial system having largely served to finance these same elections). Elections are like the black box of the political system. Input: dirty money, murky consciences, compromises, opportunism; output: a squeaky clean political situation. And the motorists' immorality is as nothing compared with the cynical way the politicians, the insiders, the financial experts and the manipulators of all kinds have cynically jumped the gun on the great electoral pardon. The criminals, fraudsters and other political and financial speculators have also unreservedly, unscrupulously pre-empted this symbolic amnesty, this liquidation of all civic criminality which the *trompe-l'oeil* democratic operation of the elections represents. Democracy, having treated its haemorrhages, its menstrual flow, with repeated scandals, regenerates in electoral coitus.

13. The tradition of incoming presidents granting amnesties on driving offences has been widely criticized for leading to increased numbers of road deaths.

Yet civic virtue still has the last word: where there are more than three points on the licence, there will be no amnesty for motorists. A happy idea, since the points-based licence is an excellent formula. It is merely scandalous that it applies only to motoring. We should expand the system and create a points-based existential licence. For every offence, misdeed or act of immoral behaviour you would have existence points docked from your licence. When the points ran out, it would be withdrawn altogether. In this way, the roadways of existence would be less crowded, with the removal of all those who cannot behave properly. You might be sent for remedial treatment under the direction of conscience experts, but otherwise the ban on living would be immediately enforceable. The points licence would just have to be inserted as a programmed implant and the offender would be 'terminated' by automatic heart-failure. This would be the full-blown application of human rights. And then we would have a clearer view of the just, unyielding application of democracy.

7 August 1995

Weep, Citizens!

Democracy is no exception to the rule that systems never function better than when running counter to their own rules and operating in spite of their own principles. This is their fundamental vice and systems, like individuals, draw their strength from their vices. Tocqueville should always be tempered with Mandeville; *Democracy in America* with the *Fable of the Bees*. It is this joyful perversity, this perpetual subversion of principles which is the most exhilarating thing about the political sphere. All the great political operations have drawn their inspiration from this. It is the end of cynical reason we should bemoan, and the advent of sentimental reason. The decline of the political sphere can be measured by the desperate attempt to identify with its own principles, and the repentance which always ensues from this in the exercise of power. The paradox of the actor also applies to the political sphere: if that sphere identifies with its own principles, as the actor identifies with his own character, the very illusion of the political – or of the theatre – is lost.

Now, the political sphere as we know it has sacrificed its own stage. By incorporating the entire population as extras in a great sentimental, demagogic groundswell of participation, it has abolished that distance which is the basic rule of the political game. The law of the greater number has been substituted for the rules of the game. The end of the theatre, the end of the political scene.

We each of us operate on an entirely immoral basis, acting, in spite of our own principles, by a set of rules we conform to spontaneously. Only incidentally do those rules coincide with the moral law; they take the form, rather, of subtle rituals which are entirely our own affair. All institutions and political systems do the same. It is with a full sense of the wrong we do that we sacrifice moral value here. Sadly, this strategy no longer applies today, when you have to be politically correct. But the contradiction with the actual operation of the system which ensues is so flagrant as to be thoroughly amusing. What is astounding is the total lack of understanding of that actual operation on the part of enlightened souls; the way the democratic consciousness denies itself and its own principles – for example, blindly and unconditionally proscribing Le Pen in just the way he treats immigrants; denouncing violence and intolerance whatever their source, but at the same time priding itself on its 'good' intolerance and openly manipulating the electoral system, as in Algeria or Denmark to ensure the right cause wins. To which we might add the daily litany of political and media discourse, wholly preoccupied with the justification of this denial of its own principles and the shameful practices of an unavowed integrism. Such is the victory by contamination, by contagion, of the Front National. *Honi soit qui mal y pense . . .*

Is it not the role of politicians to focus the chronic sickness of the social sphere on themselves – the accursed share of the social sphere, which is the essence of power – and find a political use for it? The prince's privileged role derives from the fact that he condenses in himself all the arbitrary power scattered and spread throughout society, so that society can be rid of it. If arbitrary power is not concentrated at the top, then it is everywhere in society – this is how it is in the democratic state, where such power is diffuse and endemic, with the same perverse effects as generated by crumbling empires.

Similarly, is it not the role of the 'intellectual' to concentrate in himself the accursed share of thought and purge the whole of society of it – society thereby becoming freer to balance up good and evil for itself? Is it not his role to focus the sickness of thought on himself and find a baleful use for it?

Neither intellectuals nor politicians in any way play this role any more; in no way do they take up that cynical reason Sloterdijk speaks of.[14] They see it as their role merely to express opinions, to guide, to enlighten and to rationalize. They are all for openness and transparency (the transparency of the good, obviously); they deck themselves out with moral consciences, with suffering, witness, proselytism and cruelly unremitting zeal in the treatment of sick values (they are, of course, themselves part of the sickness). They no longer claim to be representative; theirs is a self-effacing role, allowing everyone to express themselves. A senile malady this, the pious desire to shed power – including the power of speech – and hand it on to everyone else (which, in the present situation, actually adds to the burden of liberty). Of course this hypocritical *auto-da-fé* is no solution, and everyone – politicians and intellectuals alike – still dies in the end, but now they die playing someone else's role. As for society and thought, they are exposed in this way to internal confusion and virulence – literally: to the transparence of evil, which, no longer finding anywhere to manifest itself, filters everywhere into repentance, indifference and hatred.

The exercise of power always involved the risk of death. That is the price to be paid for having public life become a matter of total indifference. But, ultimately, why complain about the current deliquescence and senility of the political class? As

14. Peter Sloterdijk, *Critique of Cynical Reason* (London: Verso, 1988).

though we still believed intelligence were in power, when we have blindingly clear evidence of the opposite! We should, rather, pride ourselves on this end to the political sphere and the collusion of the political class itself in that end! It is that class, without distinction of party or faction, which is now carrying out the *fatwa* we have issued against it, the decree that it shall dissolve itself and disappear. We no longer need to attack it. It is undergoing spontaneous self-destruction. All we have to do is steadfastly refuse to assist it in its hour of need.

It is, however, a shameful end. So we are torn between the recognition of this shameful state of affairs – a shame in which we inevitably feel implicated – and secret jubilation at this death foretold. We might even suggest that the task of politicians today is to swallow the corpse of the political sphere, and we might then thank them for protecting us, like living sarcophagi, from its decay, which would otherwise invade the whole of society.

All calamities protect us from something worse. So the stupidity and blindness of politicians must have a higher function – the function of protecting us, by the thick layer of dirt and discourse they secrete, from the secret violence of the judgement which, were it not for them, we would be forced to exercise and turn against ourselves.

Above all, we should not try to correct their illusory conceptions. That would leave us exposed without protection to an unequal encounter with stupidity and with the burden of our freedom.

21 August 1995

Helots and Elites

We live in a thoroughly split political reality. On the one hand, we have the political class, a parallel micro-society which has secretly been made redundant, going about its business with impunity, and apparently doomed to perform the single task of reproducing itself in an endogamous confusion of all persuasions – the incestuous alliance of Right and Left producing an entire pathology and degeneracy characteristic of inbreeding. On the other hand, we have a 'real' society which is increasingly disconnected from the political sphere. Both of these, moving apart from each other at considerable speed, seem destined more or less to wither away or to break up each in their own little corner – drip-fed as they are solely through the umbilical of the media and the opinion polls. Virtuality – in the sense that the political will now operates only on the mental screens of TV sets and through opinion polls – has turned the political function and the political scene into more or less useless vestigial remains. No dialectic, not even a dialectic of conflict, keeps the two opposing poles interacting.

We find the same situation in the economy. On the one hand, the battered remnants of production and the real economy; on the other, the circulation of gigantic amounts of virtual capital. But the two are so disconnected that the misfortunes which beset that capital — stock market crashes and other financial debacles — do not bring about the collapse of real economies any more. It is the same in the political sphere: scandals, corruption and the general decline in standards have no decisive effects in a split society, where responsibility (the possibility that the two parties may *respond to each other*) is no longer part of the game.

This paradoxical situation is in a sense beneficial: it protects civil society (what remains of it) from the vicissitudes of the political sphere, just as it protects the economy (what remains of it) from the random fluctuations of the Stock Exchange and international finance. The immunity of the one creates a reciprocal immunity in the other — a mirror indifference. Better: real society is losing interest in the political class, while nonetheless availing itself of the spectacle. At last, then, the media have some use, and the 'society of the spectacle' assumes its full meaning in this fierce irony: the masses availing themselves of the spectacle of the dysfunctionings of representation through the random twists in the story of the political class's corruption. All that remains now to the politicians is the obligation to sacrifice themselves to provide the requisite spectacle for the entertainment of the people. For if, in the past, the principle of power involved laying your life on the line, the zero degree of power merely involves an artificial *auto-da-fé*. Once again we have cause to thank the politicians, who free us from the tiresome obligation of having to manage that empty place power has become — much as it falls to others to manage money, business, leisure, morals and culture. All superfluous tasks happily left to the charlatans, predators and speculators, not to mention the waxen-lipped philosophers.

The socialist episode will have been the finest illustration of this leukaemia of the political sphere. With political will having gone into abeyance and with the pole position of power virtually vacant (since 1968 perhaps?), the Left dashed in to take it and immediately crumbled into the void. (In the same way, with the masculine pole position virtually unoccupied – male privilege having disappeared – feminism rushed in to assume it and, naturally, fell into the trap that is the power vacuum itself.)

We should, in fact, congratulate Mitterand on doing a large part of the work: on ensuring, by a kind of posthumous sweep, the deep corruption of the whole political system, on mystifying and sweeping away the whole of the divine Left![15]

If the Left collapsed in this way, far beyond the actual point of its true decline – with it going all dreams of putting the imagination in power – this was not because it lacked any gift for exercising power or had committed any fatal errors (unfortunately, it merely accumulated banal ones), but because, in spite of the advanced brittleness of its historical bones, it proved incapable of speaking for the indifference and inertia of the social body. In a sense, it is almost to its credit that it was not able to shake off its ideals totally – even though it had given up pursuing them.

The Right, for its part, identifies spontaneously with this inert ghost of the social body and its deep resentment of the political sphere. It is, in this sense, not so much political as transpolitical – that is to say, aligned with the lowest common denominator of a politically disaffected society. It is the Right which reaps the fruits of this disaffection. But, since it also has no political perspective, the failings of Right and Left combine harmoniously.

Who spoke of putting the imagination in power? There never is any imagination in power.

15. See Jean Baudrillard, *La Gauche divine* (Paris: Grasset, 1985).

As for the type of events this split society produces, Europe is a fine example. It is the archetype of the contemporary event, the vacuum-packed event, the vacuum-packed phantasmagoria. Europe (at least the current European project) will not have happened in the heads, dreams or natural inspiration of anyone whatsoever. If it has happened, it has been in the somnambulistic space of the political will, of the dossiers and speeches, the programmes and calculations – and in that artificial synthesis of opinion that is universal suffrage, a process strictly guided and controlled by the cunning idealism of politicians and experts. Europe, as it is emerging, is, in a way, a simulation model projected into a scene of social desertification – an obligatory virtual reality, to be slipped into like a data suit (the Gulf War was already handed to us as a vacuum-packed war – also for us to slip into like virtual reality).

We shall no more be spared Europe than we shall the Internet, the single currency or the chains selling deep-frozen foods. These things happen come what may. They follow out their course in spite of any opinions to the contrary. Decisions will go on being made, circulating among the elites, experts and strategists, heedless of any collective opinion. We are totally powerless in spite of – or as a consequence of – the information in which we are steeped. We saw this in Rwanda. All the media said clearly where the killers were – the instigators (which included us) – and yet the whole business went on happening. We have total information, but it has no effect. The consensus, the collective cowardice find an alibi in this generalized news and information. Information plays the role of a scalpel, forever separating the juntas in power in all the countries of the world from any collective will, and cicatrizing, as if with hot irons, the contradictions which may ensue.

In this fracture between helots and elites, it is silly and senseless to wrap oneself in the flag of the divine Left and its democratic arrogance and deplore the stupidity of the masses, duped by the media and the electoral system – a position we have recently seen adopted towards Berlusconi in Italy or Le Pen's advances in the French local elections. That is merely a short-sighted, conventional analysis of political reason. In the end, the 'blind' masses seem to see things more subtly than the 'enlightened' intellectuals: they see that the seats of power are empty, corrupt places of despair, and hence logically one should put characters of precisely this type in them: empty individuals, buffoons, ham actors and charlatans – the ideal people for the situation. Take Berlusconi for example. The political world, as it is, represents the only possible 'real' – even if it is not rational. If you want to change something, then you have to set about reality itself, which is quite another matter. Berlusconi and Le Pen are what they are, and all recriminations against the 'irrational' masses are merely the product of a naive illuminism (both cunning and politically correct). However, it is equally undeniable that we find this state of affairs unbearable – whether it be Berlusconi, Le Pen or the current deliquescent state of politics. We have, then, to come to terms with a contradictory situation in that we both have the system we deserve and – equally non-negligibly – we cannot bear it. This is a form of insoluble dilemma. You can have a visceral anti-mass, anti-yob, anti-redneck reaction. But an equally visceral anti-elite, anti-caste, anti-culture, anti-*nomenklatura* reaction. Should you be on the side of the mindless masses or of arrogant privilege (arrogant particularly in claiming an affinity with the masses)? There is no solution. We are caught between two integrisms: the one populist (or Islamic and fundamentalist), the other liberal and elitist, the integrism of enforced democracy and the universal. For this latter an Enlightenment fanaticism which no longer knows what values to subscribe to, the other form – the populist, Islamic type – provides a providential target. But it is itself a fanaticism, which Islamic fundamentalism, with equal intolerance, does not recognize as having a moral and political right to exist. And the two operate against the same backdrop of an indifferent New World Order. Is there still a place between the two for a pro-fane practice of freedom?

4 September 1995

Information at the
Meteorological Stage

Information long ago broke through the truth barrier and moved into the hyper-space where things are neither true nor false, since everything in the realm of information depends on instantaneous credibility. Or, to put it more accurately, information is truer than true *since it is true in real time* – this is why it is funda-mentally uncertain. Or again, to draw on Mandelbrot's recent theory, we can say that things in the information space or the historical space, like those in fractal space, are no longer one-, two- or three-dimensional: they float in some inter-mediate dimension. We no longer have any standards of truth or objectivity, but a scale of probability.

You put out an item of information. So long as it has not been denied, it is plausible. And, barring some happy accident, it will never be denied in real time and so will always remain credible. Even if denied, it will no longer ever be absolutely false, since it has once been credible. Unlike truth, credibility has no limits; it cannot be refuted, because it is virtual. We are in a kind of *fractal truth*: just as a fractal object no longer has one, two or three dimensions (in whole numbers), but 1.2 or 2.3 dimensions, so an event is no longer necessarily true or false, but hovers between 1.2 or 2.3 octaves of truth. The space between the true and the false is no longer a relational space, but a space of random distribution.

We could, of course, say the same of the space between good and evil, beauty and ugliness, cause and effect. Even sexuality today moves in a curious intermediate dimension – neither masculine nor feminine – but at 1.5 or 1.7 somewhere between the two (hence the impossibility of operating with the concept of sexual difference, from lack of definition). The uncertainty principle does not belong to physics alone; it is at the heart of all our actions, at the heart of 'reality'.

This erratic situation, this lack of moorings and generalized uncertainty, is shifting all facts, events and their interpretation into a phase or stage we might term *meteorological*. Yet this is no longer the stage of the natural unpredictability of the elements, of wind and weather, but of a secondary undecidability, arising from the very perfection of calculations and information.

Take the TV weather forecast. The presenters have turned this into a game show. From the satellite data, which serve as a scientific alibi, they seek the ideal formula: the words which will satisfy the public without being too wide of the actual events. They are caught between the instability of atmospheric flows and the instability of collective expectations, which makes the forecast virtually a political matter. They try more or less consciously, on a daily basis, to cobble the two things together into ephemeral simulation models. So, news of the weather can run precisely counter to what you see out of your window, but it is true *in simulation*, since it is deduced from the various data of a model scenario. Which involves many other factors besides meteorological considerations. The presenter will take account of the errors in the previous day's forecast, of the consideration that the weather cannot be bad three weekends running (the population would not stand for it) and naturally also the objective fact of the approach of a depression or anti-cyclone – but this fact, which so often turns out to be wrong, cannot be determinant in the forecast. It follows that the degree of pertinence of the weather forecast is, taken overall, less than that of normal intuition. As a result, to the poetic uncertainty of the skies we must daily add the arbitrary uncertainty of meteorological discourse.

Yet we are told that it is going to be possible, using ultra-sophisticated computer techniques, to make an accurate forecast of the weather over the next two days. But the computers will take four days to do it. So in four days' time we shall know precisely what the weather was on the preceding two days. The truth of the forecast has no concern with *truly* being a *fore*cast. And the facts simply have to fall into line. If necessary, truth will correct them retrospectively. It will have been fine even if it rained. For facts are facts and truth is truth. It always arrives too late, but when it does arrive it is truth which commands belief.

It is no accident that in all the media the weather bulletin always directly precedes or follows the stock market report. The incoherence of stock exchange movements is a fitting counterpart to the fluctuations of weather computations. To which we can add the many opinion polls, which obey the same logic at the level of public opinion.

If we may hypothesize a reality of economic activity, a reality of weather and a reality of public opinion, whatever it may be, then the version given to us through the Stock Exchange, the weather forecasts and the opinion polls is a purely speculative one, which only distantly reflects the realities concerned. There is doubtless some kind of strategy behind this transcription in simulated form, but, as with fashion, no one can tell who gains by it. No one can claim to exploit the opinion polls – not even those who believe they manipulate them. As for the purposes of the Stock Exchange, they are unintelligible. You get the worrying feeling that this undecidability, this floating of rates, prices and exchange rates must have a meaning and a purpose, but for whom and for what? In our perverse system of government, it is, at any rate, a powerful wellspring of collective uncertainty and disillusionment. It is a transpolitical form of destabilization of the social body.

For if meteorology is becoming, in a way, political, politics is becoming meteorological. As much play is made of figures, co-efficients, rates and indices as of the random movements of the heavens; and periods of depression and high pressure alternate in the field of events and opinion with the same regularity as in the stratosphere.

It even seems that, by a supreme irony, reality is now beginning to conform to these (misplaced) speculations. Opinion is beginning to merge with the polls; or at any rate there is virtually no other mirror of public opinion but the polls (there is a good reason for this: namely, that, as Bourdieu says, public opinion does not exist). The real economy is now coming to merge with the mirror of the Stock Exchange, where it assumes its ultimate face as instantaneous flow, as a limitless operation with no precise goal, a collective spectacle. Little by little, the kind of fluctuations which occur on the Stock Exchange – of buying and selling, transference and dumping, loss-making speculation and forward-trading – has invaded the production and management sectors of the real economy.

It seems that everything – even the weather – has wearily come round to complying with the models, and has meekly become as incoherent as the weather forecast. It is as though the forecasts had finally unsettled the weather, in much the same way as financial speculation ends up modifying economic processes and polls end up obsessing and obscuring public opinion. There can be no doubt that reality is driven into turmoil on contact with models, or ends up ironically conforming to them, like the dreams and unconscious of primitive peoples on contact with psycho-anthropologists. One thing is certain: meteorology has become a reference scenario. So long as the wind was blowing in the direction of the rational and the predictable across all disciplines, from the human to the exact sciences, meteorology remained the emblem of the unpredictable, the uncontrollable element of our daily lives, and, as a result, the subject of perpetual comment (secret marvelling at the weather).

But now that the same disciplines – from physics to economics, from cosmogony to sociology, from biology to history – are going over, if not to the irrational, then at least to the uncertainty principle, to calculations of probability, to flexible hypotheses, floating verification and the reversibility of propositions, the meteorological realm is becoming the mirror of their uncertainty, the paradigm for their absence of moorings. What was once pleasant climatic fantasy has developed into a prophetic approximation of the new kind of events by which we are beset. The promotion of the random, the accidental and the insignificant in analysis – such as the promotion of the *fait divers* in sociology or the slip in psychology – is not new.

The anomaly is becoming a source of understanding, as is everything which is an exception to the rule. Why should this not also apply to weather events? Is it not marvellous that our most sophisticated calculations turn out to be as uncertain as the unpredictability of the weather? Is it not the most attractive feature of politicians that their strategies turn out in the end to be the equivalent of stratospheric events?

This restores to all fields – politics among them – a suspense which disappeared long ago. The only events today run *counter to* statistics (similarly, only what runs *counter to* politics and *counter to* history constitutes an event today). For people who no longer have any opinion, and who do not in any event have any chance of making it count – hemmed in as they are by discourses even before they are hemmed in by figures – the stakes are shifting from the ideological terrain to the statistical. And the only pleasure, the only hope – sometimes fulfilled – is to prove the pollsters wrong, to have one's choices and acts produce some other outcome than the one anticipated. A collective evil genius is at work here. In a game as tiresome as politics, the only interesting event is the statistical reversal of the situation (as, for example, in 1992 with the French referendum on Europe). The fickleness of the statistical masses, not unlike the capricious movement of clouds, reduced the opinion polls to a kind of lottery and, through that lottery, brought democracy itself down to a kind of random game, elevating the uncertainty principle – as in Babylon or with the horse races in Byzantium – to the status of a rule.

18 September 1995

Disembodied Violence: Hate[16]

Hate: instead of deploring the resurgence of an atavistic violence, we should see that it is our modernity itself, our hypermodernity which produces this type of violence, and these special effects. Indeed, terrorism is part of this too. Traditional violence is much more enthusiastic and sacrificial. Ours is a simulated violence in the sense that it wells up, not so much from passion and instinct, but from the screen. It is, in a sense, potentially present in the screen and the media, which pretend to record it and broadcast it, but which in reality precede it and prompt it. As everywhere else, the media here precede this violence, as they do terrorist acts. This is what makes it a specifically modern form; and this too is why it is impossible to assign real (political, sociological or psychological) causes to it. One senses that all explanations of that type are deficient. Similarly, it makes little sense to berate the media for propagating violence by showing it or telling violent stories. For the screen, a virtual surface, protects us rather well, whatever is said about it, from the real contents of the image. Because of the way the screen breaks the cycle, violence

16. Mathieu Kassovitz's film *La Haine* (Hate) was released in France in March 1995.

in films and TV does not lead on to behavioural violence. It is the violence of the medium itself which leaves us defenceless – the violence of the virtual and its non-spectacular proliferation. What is to be feared is not the psychological spread of violence, but its technological extension – the extension of a transparent violence, the kind which leads to the disembodiment of all reality and referentiality: the degree Xerox of violence.

It is because our society no longer allows space for real violence, historical or class violence, that it generates a virtual, reactive violence. A phantom violence as it were, the way we speak of a phantom pregnancy, a violence which, like that phantom condition, gives birth to nothing whatever, neither founds nor generates anything whatever. 'Hate' is like this. One might regard it as an archaic impulse, but, paradoxically, because it is disconnected from its object and its ends, it is con-temporaneous with the hyperreality of the great metropolises. We may distinguish a basic form of violence, the violence of aggression, oppression, rape, domination, humiliation and spoliation – the unilateral violence of the strongest. And this might find a reply in a contradictory violence – historical violence, critical violence, the violence of the negative. Ruptural, transgressive violence (to which we may add the violence of analysis, the violence of interpretation). These are forms of deter-minate violence, with an origin and an end, and their causes and effects can be identified. They correspond to a transcendence, whether it be the transcendence of power, history or meaning.

Against this there stands opposed a properly contemporary form of violence. More subtle than the violence of aggression: a violence of deterrence, pacification, neutralization, control – a violence of quiet extermination, a genetic, communica-tional violence – the violence of the consensus and conviviality which tends to abolish – through drugs, disease prevention, psychical and media regulation – the very roots of evil and hence of all radicality. The violence of a system which roots out any form of negativity and singularity (including the ultimate form of singularity – death itself). The violence of a society in which negativity is virtually prohibited, conflict is prohibited, death is prohibited. A violence which, in a way, puts an end to violence itself. A violence which can be met by no equal and opposite violence. Only hate.

Born of indifference – particularly the indifference radiated by the media – hate is a cool, discontinuous form, which can switch instantly to any object. It is not heated and it lacks conviction; it is consumed in the process of its acting-out – and often in its image and the immediate repercussions – as can be seen from the current outbursts of delinquency on the big city estates. If traditional violence reflected the level of oppression and conflict, hate reflects the level of consensus and conviviality. Our eclectic culture is the culture of the mingling of opposites, the co-existence of all differences within a great cultural melting pot. But let us not have any illusions about this: it is precisely this multiculturalism, this tolerance, this synergy, which stir up the temptation of a general abreaction, a gut rejection. Synergy produces allergy. Over-protection leads to a loss of defences and immunity: the redundant anti-bodies turn around against the organism itself. Hate is of this order: like many modern diseases, it has something of self-aggression and auto-immune pathology about it. We are not yet ready to cope with the condition of artificial immunity which our big cities provide for us. We are like a species whose natural predators have been removed – doomed either very quickly to disappear or to destroy itself. In a sense, we use hate to protect ourselves from this lack of the other, the enemy or opposition – with hate mobilizing a kind of artificial, object-less oppositionality. In this way, hate is a kind of 'fatal strategy' against the pacification of existence. In its very ambiguity, it is a desperate protest against the indifference of our world and doubtless, for that reason, a much more intense mode of relation than consensus or conviviality.

The contemporary transition from violence to hate is characteristic of the shift from an object passion to an objectless passion. A pure and undifferentiated violence, a violence of a third type, as it were, contemporaneous with the exponential violence of the terrorist and with all the viral, epidemic forms of contagion and chain reaction. Hate is more unreal, more elusive in its manifestations than straight violence. You can see this clearly in racism and delinquency. This is why it is so difficult to counter it, either by prevention or police crackdowns. You cannot de-motivate it, since it has no explicit motivation. You can't demobilize it, since it has no clear mobilizing factor. And it is none too easy to punish it, since most of the time it takes itself as the target: it is, pre-eminently, a passion at odds with itself.

We seem doomed to reproduce the Same in an endless identification, in a universal culture of identity, and this gives rise to an enormous resentment: self-hatred. Not hatred of the other, as a superficial interpretation of racism would have it, but the loss of the other and resentment of that loss. The usual contention is that hate is a hatred of the other – hence the illusion one is opposing it by preaching tolerance and respect for difference – but in fact hate (racism, etc.) is not so much a rejection of the other as a *fanatical desire for otherness*. It seeks despairingly to compensate for the loss of the other by the exorcizing of an artificial other, which may, as a result, be anyone whatever. In a lobotomized world, where conflicts are immediately contained, it seeks to resuscitate otherness – if only to destroy it. It seeks to escape that fateful identification, that autistic confinement to which the very movement of our culture condemns us. This is a culture of *Ressentiment*, then, but one in which, behind the resentment of the other, one cannot but sense a resentment of self, of the dictatorship of the self and the selfsame, which may extend as far as self-destruction.

So we must see 'hate', in all its ambiguity, as a crepuscular passion – simultaneously symptom and operator of this sudden loss of the social, of otherness, of conflict and, lastly, of the system itself, threatened with gravitational collapse. A symptom of the end or the failure of modernity – if not the end of history, for paradoxically there has never been any end of history, since there has never been a resolution of all the problems it has posed. There is, rather, a passing beyond the end, without anything having been resolved. And in the current 'hate', there is precisely a resentment of everything that has not taken place. And, with this, the urgent desire to hurry things on so as to be done with the system, to bring something else into being, to conjure up the other, the event from elsewhere. In this cool fanaticism, one can glimpse a millenarian form of provocation.

We've all 'got hate'. It is more than we could manage not to. We are all ambiguously nostalgic for the end of the world, that is to say, wanting to give it an end, some end-goal, at any price – if only through resentment and total rejection of the world as it is.

2 October 1995

Psychedelic Violence: Drugs

Drugs in general no longer play a part in the symbolic rituals of the industrialized societies. These societies are given over to deferred goals which assume a calculated sacrifice of time and energy, whereas drug-use always presupposes the immediacy of a mental process and a kind of achieved utopia. Throughout the ages, all thinking which has advocated the immediate achievement of utopia has been condemned as heretical.

In the view we take of modern drugs, something of this ancestral condemnation remains, together with something of the occult power drugs derive from their ancient virtues. We may say, then, that they fascinate as much as they repel, and that, from the standpoint of Western reason, they are definitively ambivalent. They have a narcotic effect on the body and the brain – and also on the way we judge them.

In our present-day analysis, it has long been customary to see drugs as relating to 'anomie' in Durkheim's sense. In this, they are akin to a certain type of suicide which characterizes the social bodies of the industrialized countries. These are residual, marginal, transgressive forms, forms which lie outside the law, beyond the general social organization and system of organic values of the group. It is a matter of margins, but of margins which do not challenge the principle of the law and of value and can potentially be integrated into the cycle of the law and values.

The current status of drugs is, in fact, quite different. In common with certain other specifically contemporary phenomena, it is not anomic, but *anomalous*. The anomalous is not what is marginal, unbalanced or organically in deficit; it is the product of an excess of organization, regulation and rationalization within a system. It is that which for no apparent reason comes, seemingly from outside, to disrupt the operation of the system. It is that which comes from the very logic, the excess of logic and rationality, of a system which, once it has reached a certain saturation threshold, secretes its antibodies, its internal pathologies, its strange dysfunctions, its unforeseeable, incurable accidents, its *anomalies*.

This is no longer the effect of a society's inability to integrate its margins, but rather of an over-capacity for integration and normalization. It is at this point that societies which are apparently omnipotent are destabilized from within – and this involves serious consequences, for the more the system attempts to resolve its anomalies, the more it will enter the logic of over-organization and the more it will fuel their eccentric growth.

We have to leave rationalist conceptions behind here. In the past, the anomic margins provided an occasion for increased rationalization of the system. Today it is the over-rationalization of the system which causes anomalous accidents and aggravates them.

We have to take this 'perverse' logic into account and distinguish between a drug-use linked to inadequate social and economic development (which is still often found in the developing countries or among the underprivileged) and a form of use linked, rather, to the saturation of the world of consumption – as both apogee and parody of that same consumption, as a contestatory anomaly of a world one has to escape from because it is *too abundant*, not because it could be said to lack something.

We are thus dealing here with what might be described as a drug-use of a 'second type'. And we should see this in terms of all those processes of a 'second type' contemporaneous with it – processes which obey this same anomalous logic. In particular, forms of violence of the 'second type' – forms which are not of the order of primary offending behaviour or aggression, but born of a reaction to the industrialized societies' excessive tolerance, the over-protection of the social body. Terrorism is of this order. It is a response to the omnipotence of modern states, which secrete it not as historic violence, but as anomalous violence, which they cannot stamp out, other than by turning themselves into even more controlled, more detersive, more powerful states, and so continuing the upward spiral.

Such pathologies of the 'second type' as AIDS and cancer are also of this order. These are no longer traditional illnesses caused by the organic deficiency of bodies exposed to external attack; they result rather from a destabilization of over-protected bodies (all the hygienic, chemical, medical, social and psychological prosthetics) which, as a result, lose their immunity and fall prey to any old virus. And just as there is apparently no 'political' solution to the problem of terrorism, there does not for the moment seem to be any biomedical solution to the problem of AIDS and cancer – and for the same reason. The fact is that these are anomalous processes, which precisely run counter – with a savage, reactional violence – to the political or biological over-protection of the social body or the physical one.

The use and abuse of drugs is part of this same symptomatology. We may condemn the existence of this curse and the behaviour which goes with it, but what we can be sure of is that the society which seeks to root it out and expunge it once and for all from the social body is running a very great risk. Now, the desire to do this exists; it is even part of the rationalist paranoia of our social systems. We have to weigh up the serious deficit we incur because of drugs, but we must also weigh up the serious deficit or deficiency that would result from their elimination. This is how we generate cancers or viruses which are much more cunning, and which do not even have the mitigating charm of accursedness.

The point where collective loss of immune defences or individual loss of symbolic defences occurs is the point where some societies become vulnerable to terrorism, drugs or violence (but also to depression and fascism). And we can easily see that the only solution lies in restoring these immunities or symbolic defences. But we know that our system tends, in the very name of science and progress, to destroy all natural immunities and substitute artificial immune systems – prosthetics – for them. What hope is there that such a system will do anything other than continue in this same direction? With this, we can suddenly see drug-use from a quite different angle, which is directly contrary to what has so far been argued: while being part of the syndrome of immunodeficiency, drugs are themselves a defence. There are doubtless better defences, but it is not inconceivable that this use and abuse represent a vital, symbolic reaction – though an apparently desperate and suicidal one – to something even worse.

Without subscribing to the 'feel-good' ideology of the sixties and seventies on the 'mind-expanding powers of drugs', we may still take the – rather more prosaic – view that there is here something of an escape from the objective drudgery of life in some societies, a communal reflex of misbehaviour in the face of universal normalization, rationalization and programming, which are undoubtedly an even graver danger to society and the species in the long term. We know that human beings gain effective protection from madness by resorting to neurosis.

Similarly, it is not by good, but by relative evil that one can protect oneself from absolute evil. The Church has understood how to manage its heresies in this same way – as necessary (from its point of view) aberrations, as pernicious germs of something (but germs all the same). A Church which no longer gives rise to heresies, or which has eliminated them all, eventually withers away, just as a body which stops producing germs, including those working to destroy it, is a dead body.

Having said this, drug-use is no longer in its intensive phase, the phase in which it was supported by a euphoric or heroic, subversive or suicidal discourse. It is in its extensive phase. And if it is spreading further, it is, as a result, losing some of its violence. Drug-use is no longer a subversive anomie, but an anomaly becoming institutionalized.

So should we crack down on it more than ever? A new hard anti-drug line may seem problematic (when there is no pro-drug discourse). In the fragile state of equilibrium or disequilibrium in which the immune system of the social or individual body finds itself, that hard line would introduce a rigid moralizing element, a legal rigidity which is no longer appropriate in the delicate management of anomalies (and this is all the more ambiguous in that it often provides a cover for political strategies for which drugs, like any other form of offending behaviour, provide an easy alibi).

The problem of drug-use must be treated *delicately*, and (since it is an ambiguous problem) with strategies which are themselves ambiguous. Above all, unilateral strategies of denunciation, which simply bolster the hypocrisy of a certain type of society, are to be avoided, as are strategies of differentiating between use and abuse, since no one could specify the shifting limits between the two. Drugs – all drugs – are forms of exorcistic behaviour: they exorcize reality, the social order, the indifference of things. But through drugs, it is society itself which exorcizes certain forgotten powers, drives and internal contradictions. It is society which produces this perverse effect and society which condemns it. If it is not going to stop producing the effect, then it should at least stop cursing it.

UNESCO

The Dark Continent of Childhood

There is now within the social and political order a specific problem of childhood. A problem inseparable from those of sexuality, drugs, violence, hatred and all the insoluble problems posed by social exclusion. Like so many other areas, childhood and adolescence are today becoming spaces doomed by abandonment to marginality and delinquency.

The news offers a daily chronicle of this violence: adolescents murdering their parents, violence of children against other children, violence among inner city youth, this latter still taking a relatively socialized form in gangs. But there are also cases of purely individual 'acting out' (with the youngster from Cuers, a child has for the first time entered the annals of mass killers). All these episodes are inexplicable in simple psychological, social or moral terms. There is something else going on here, which arises out of the very breakdown of the biological and symbolic orders.

To begin with, the status of birth has been turned upside down (after the status of death, which is unrecognizable today in properly human terms). Artificial insemination in all its forms, genetic control and manipulation: everywhere birth seems in danger of being deflected from its natural destiny into an artificial one. The liquidation in the long term of a familial, sexual genesis, of a psychical and biological begetting. It is the end of the child as bearer not only of the duality of a man and a woman, but the duality of a past and a future, which alone creates a memory. As a result, the child becomes a technical performance, a mini-extension of the parents, rather than a genuine 'other'. A sort of by-product of an incestuous doubling – ultimately not unlike the scissiparity or schizogenesis of protozoa – conceived as an ideal outgrowth in your image: the clone-child, whose production from the DNA of a single one of your cells is currently being planned. As a technical operation this is as yet some way off, but it is already present in the scientific and collective imaginary – and even in the relationship between parents and their children.

In fact, the child is no longer a child. Children are substitute beings, who are losing their natural otherness and entering upon a satellite existence on the artificial orbit of sameness. They will find it increasingly difficult to detach themselves; to find, not their identity and their autonomy – as they are constantly being told they must – but their distance and their strangeness. The more genetic heredity is foregrounded, the more the symbolic heritage disappears. Even the Oedipal drama is not played out any longer. There is no longer any resolution of childhood, since the psychical and symbolic conditions of childhood no longer even exist. Childhood is losing even the chance of surpassing and denying itself as such. It is disappearing as a phase in the metamorphosis of the human being. At the same time as it is losing this distinctive spirit of its own and its singularity, it is becoming a sort of dark continent.

For otherness inevitably re-emerges, but differently, in the form of a vast, shady complicity on the part of a generation which is at last free from adult attention, but is no longer minded to grow up. An endless, purposeless adolescence, which is acquiring autonomy with no reference to the Other, acquiring it for itself – and turning, in some cases violently, against the Other, against the adult with whom it now has no sense either of descendance or solidarity. This is no longer a symbolic break, but a pure and simple rejection, which may find expression in a lethal 'acting out'. And it is not even 'acting out', since that still presupposes the irruption of the phantasm into a real world, whereas here we are dealing with an infantile, quasi-hallucinatory state which reaches back before the reality principle. Moreover, this pre-reality-principle, infantile state coincides strangely with the world of virtual reality, our adult media world, the post-reality-principle world, in which the real and the virtual merge.

This explains the spontaneous affinity of the entire younger generation with the new virtual technologies. The child has a special relationship with the instantaneous. Music, electronics, drugs – all these things are immediately familiar to him. Psychedelic isolation does not frighten him. Where real time is concerned, he is way ahead of the adult, who cannot but seem a retard to him, just as in the field of moral values, he cannot but seem a fossil.

So the child enters a state of anomie, of organic desocialization. But even when 'naturally' produced, he has become an anomaly. He is out of time. The current tempo, based on immediacy, acceleration, 'real time', runs precisely counter to generation, gestation, the time of bearing and raising, the long haul in general, which is the duration of human childhood. The child is, then, logically condemned to disappear. Other methods ought to make it possible for us to do without this natural maturation of the human being, a process which is so long and the source of so many neuroses, of conflicts which few modern couples can withstand, and which was designed for a situation of generational continuity, where there were long-term transgenerational rituals in place. Today, the general quickening of the pace of life condemns childhood to accelerated obsolescence.

Let us take some comfort, however, from the fact that there will always be children, though as objects of curiosity or sexual perversion, or compassion, or pedagogical manipulation and experimentation, or quite simply as vestiges of a genealogy of living beings – just as there will always be thoroughbred horses or pets, or works of art, as protected species or reserves, even when the natural species long since died out. They will be preserved in the same way as animals, which will soon have no other purpose than to be preserved and kept in museums as traces of the genesis of man (man himself being destined for the status of future remnant in a world of clones). So the child, the child concept, will be fetishized. It already is: idealized and fetishized as a vestige of a species whose reproduction – become progressively a technical operation – no longer in any sense involves a sexed destiny, nor the marvellously accidental product of that destiny, the child.

You only have to look at the Universal Declaration of the Rights of the Child, adopted by the UN, to know that childhood is already an endangered species: 'I can say no . . . I have the right to know who I am . . . I have the right to suitable and balanced food . . . Everyone must protect me against mental and physical violence . . . I have the right to sing, dance, play and develop my gifts for my greater happiness, etc.' (Never has there been a more Ubu-esque declaration; moreover, it makes a mockery of children, turning them into performing monkeys by foisting upon them the legalistic mania of adults.)

So children will be exorcized as natural beings, as anachronistic survivals from another age in a time of immediate optimal performance. Simultaneously, they will become a wild, delinquent, criminal species. They will lose the belief that they are children, ceasing to compare themselves pejoratively with the adult model. Doubtless they have always been potentially dangerous beings – a reality concealed by pedagogy and the modern, bourgeois idealization of childhood – and they have always taken revenge for their inferiority in their own way, through ruse and blackmail, but that subordination and revenge were merely relative because they were always doomed to disappear – with time. But now it is time which childhood is not going to have, and the evolutionary chain is broken: the child is going to turn against the adult as an all-out enemy. He will become the Other, all the same, but now the other as *Alien* – a monster produced by the breakdown in the symbolic chain of the generations.

Reality was the reality of the adult (not even this is true today when he is no longer the master of it). Childhood, from the depths of its unreality, the depths of its *idiotie*, was one of the last bastions of the poetic illusion of the world. Like all other forms of illusion, it is doomed to disappear sooner or later – or to lead a purely auxiliary existence. This is the child no longer in any sense as destiny, as the accident bearing death as well as jubilation for the parents, but the child as commodity, unfortunately unintegratable into the cycle of accelerated exchange and hence become a non-standard product, an item from another age, floating most of the time between parents who no longer know what to do with it.

But which, like the dead, like women, like the masses, like the object, like all the categories expelled from the dominant reason, still has all it needs to take its revenge and pose an insoluble problem for the masters of reality.

16 October 1995

The Double Extermination

Today we do not think the virtual, the virtual thinks us. And to us this elusive transparency, which separates us definitively from the real, is as unintelligible as is the window pane to the fly which bangs against it without understanding what separates it from the outside world. The fly cannot even imagine what is setting this limit on its space. Similarly, we cannot even imagine how much the virtual – as though running ahead of us – has already transformed all the representations we have of the world. We cannot imagine this, for it is the particularity of the virtual that it puts an end not just to reality, but to the imagining of the real, the political and the social; not just to the reality of time, but to the imagining of the past and the future (this is what is known, in a kind of black humour, as 'real time'). So we are far from having understood that information's entry on the scene spelt an end to the unfolding of history, that the coming of artificial intelligence spelt an end to thought, etc. The illusion we still harbour about all these traditional categories – including our illusion of 'opening ourselves up to the virtual', as if it were a real extension of all potentialities – is the illusion of the fly unflaggingly banging up against the window pane. For we still believe in the *reality* of the virtual, whereas the virtual has already virtually scrambled all the pathways of thought. To shed a little light on this confusion, I shall take the most delicate example – most delicate precisely because it arises out of the most horrifying, unintelligible event in our modern history: the holocaust and those who deny it. The holocaust denial proposition is, in itself, absurd. This is so obvious that the crucial question becomes: why is there any need to plead the truth against the holocaust-deniers? Why can the question of the existence of the gas chambers even be raised? In other ages it never could have been. Those who contest holocaust denial never ask themselves why such denial is possible; they content themselves with vehement indignation. Now, the very fact of having to defend the historical reality of the gas chambers as a moral cause, of having to defend 'reality' in general by a kind of political commitment, attests sufficiently to the change in register which has occurred where historical truth is concerned, and to the ways in which objectivity has been disrupted.

Where the holocaust-deniers are plainly absurd and wrong is when they themselves espouse realism and contest *the objective, historical reality* of the holocaust. In historical time, the event took place and the evidence is there. But we are no longer in historical time; we are now in *real time*, and in real time there is no longer any evidence of anything whatever. The holocaust will never be verified in real time. Holocaust denial is, therefore, absurd in its own logic, but by its very absurdity it sheds light on the irruption of another dimension, paradoxically termed 'real time' – a dimension in which, paradoxically, objective reality disappears. And not just the reality of the present event, but also that of past and future events. Everything now runs out its course in a state of simultaneity, so that acts no longer find their meaning, effects no longer find their cause, and history can no longer be an object of reflection.

Real time is a kind of black hole into which nothing penetrates without losing its substance. In fact, the extermination camps themselves become virtual in real time, and show up only on the virtual screen. All testimony, including *Holocaust* and *Shoah*, sinks, in spite of itself – in spite of us – into the same virtual abyss – the abyss of *events* or facts which exist for as long as they exist and that is all. This is not to argue that the testimonies themselves, in their absolute sincerity, and the films (as images fully exhausting horror in the present time of the image) do not themselves contribute to this impossibility of memory: *the real holocaust is doomed to that other extermination which is that of the virtual.* This is the true final solution. So the holocaust-denial argument can no longer be truly refuted since everything and all of us – including those who reject the argument – have gone over, whether we like it or not, into an age when there is no longer any objective recourse. We are, therefore, condemned to oppose it in a kind of mirror denial, and this is indeed the undoing or defeat of thought, of historical thought and critical thought – but in fact it is not *its* defeat: it is the victory of real time over the present, over the past, over any form of logical articulation of reality whatsoever.

This destabilization of truth may be verified (so to speak) in many other cases. The O. J. Simpson affair, for example. Apart from any political or juridical considerations, we saw the trial build up into an autonomous event, following out its own media script in a stupefying way, mirroring itself in its own closed loop. As it did so, it eclipsed the real event of the murder and secreted its own truth wholly unrelated to the objective truth of the facts, for which the evidence was there. But the true guilt of Simpson may very well coincide – in this unhinging of truth from its model – with his virtual innocence. To the point that Simpson himself must no longer know exactly – once again in the real time of the trial – whether he is guilty or not. Or whether, like Oedipus, he can 'sincerely' set in train investigations to discover the criminal – who may perhaps be himself.

Even the future is not assured in real time (this was the meaning of the paradoxical proposition: 'The Year 2000 will not take place').[17] And it would seem appropriate here to discuss Paul Virilio's vision of the 'final Accident', the 'Accident to end all Accidents', the 'Apocalypse of the Virtual' which he foresees at the end of this evolution – or, better, involution – of our world into real time. Yet nothing could be less sure than that apocalypse (alas, even this certainty eludes us!). To dream of the 'final Accident' is to succumb to the illusion of the end. It is to forget that virtuality itself is virtual and that, by definition, its definitive advent, its apocalypse, cannot take on the force of reality. There will be no apocalypse of the virtual and of real time precisely because real time abolishes linear time and duration, and thereby the dimension in which they might develop to their extreme limits. There is no linear-exponential function of the Accident – any more than such a function exists for anything else – and its possible eventuation remains a random matter. The radical break with the real which the virtual creates, the black-out or collapse of time which real time brings about, happily preserve us from the ultimate extermination. The virtual system, like any other, is doomed, as it expands, to destroy its own conditions of possibility.

We should not dream, then, of an apocalypse in the future, any more indeed than we should dream of any utopia whatsoever: they will never take place in real time: they will run out of time itself.

If there is a virtual revolution, then we should accord it its full meaning and think through all its consequences, even if we remain free radically to reject it. If there is no virtual apocalypse, but the apocalypse is itself virtual (and, virtually, we are in the apocalypse: you only have to see the devastation of the real world all around), then it is the same with all the other categories. The social, the political, the historical – even the moral and psychological – *there are no longer any but virtual events within all*

17. See Jean Baudrillard, *The Illusion of the End* (Cambridge: Polity, 1994), p. 9.

these categories. This means it is useless searching for a politics *of* the virtual, an ethics *of* the virtual, etc., since it is politics itself which is becoming virtual, ethics itself which has become virtual, in the sense that both politics and ethics are losing the principles governing their action, losing their force of reality. And this even applies where technology is concerned: we speak of 'technologies of the virtual', but the truth is that there are now only – or there will soon only be – virtual technologies. Now, there can no longer be any notion of artifice in a world in which thought itself, intelligence, is becoming artificial. It is in this sense that we can say that it is the Virtual which thinks us, not the other way around.

This enquiry into the virtual is made even more delicate and complex today by the extraordinary hype surrounding it. The excess of information, the massive advertising effort, the technological pressure, the media, the infatuation or panic – everything is contributing to a kind of collective hallucination of the virtual and its effects. Windows 95, the Internet, the information superhighways – these things are already consumed in advance in discourse and fantasy. Perhaps it is a way of short-circuiting their effects to unleash them in this way in the imagination. But we are not even sure of that. Aren't hype and brainwashing themselves part of the virtual? We don't know. This is still the story of the fly banging its head against the incomprehensible fact of the window pane.

'Certitude does not exist', says a piece of New York graffiti. Beneath which has been written, 'Are you sure?'

6 November 1995

'Lost from View' and Truly Disappeared

The story of the illusionist who has a fine act making things vanish – rabbits, snakes, scarves and the like – and yet dreams of just one thing: making the woman who shares the stage with him disappear. He has tried all he knows, but to no avail. One day, however, in the middle of a banal conjuring trick, there is a burst of rapturous applause. He turns around, amazed, to see that the woman has disappeared. He does not know how he did it, or how to get her back. He will spend his whole life looking for the key to that disappearance, the secret of that spell.

In his own way, Jacques Pradel is also a TV illusionist, a virtuoso of disappearing tricks. Under cover of searching for missing persons, what does he do in his TV show *Perdu de vue* but make us vanish?[18] He shows us we are all potential 'missing persons', just as, to the police, we are all potential suspects. He reveals to us – hidden as he is behind the screen and the images – that the real 'missing persons' are the millions of TV viewers looking on dumbfounded at his sleight of hand and

18. *Perdu de vue* ran from November 1991 to 1999 on the French TF1 channel. Over that period it claimed to have reunited thousands of people with their friends and loved ones.

identifying for all they are worth with the object of the search, hoping against hope that *they* will be discovered and wrenched from their non-existence. So they are the people who are truly 'not around any more'. And the programme's more or less failed demonstration (but that is of no importance; it is always simulated) plunges them back for another week into the nothingness of their anonymity.

'We are all missing persons' the programme might be called. And in this sense – though in this sense alone – the programme is blindingly obvious. Like all the most 'mass-market' television, whose message (which is much more edifying than that of 'high-brow' television) is very clear, though initially indecipherable: 'We are all potential defectives, potential victims or terrorists, potential sufferers from AIDS or muscular dystrophy'.[19] And this is true. But, first and foremost, we are missing persons. And if we had to put Pradel's programme under the microscope, to draw some lesson from it, it would tell us: 'We all know something essential has disappeared, but we don't know what'. And Pradel pretends to be looking for a Mr X or a Mrs Y, but in reality no one gives a damn and no one is fooled. In reality, it is the real which has disappeared and behind Mr X or Mrs Y it is the disappearance of the real which fascinates people.

This is, in fact, the most important event in modern history and everyone is an actor in that event by the very fact of being there in front of their TV screens: they lost sight of the real at exactly the same time as they lost sight of themselves.

Fortunately, there are lots of other modes of disappearance and one of the most interesting aesthetic forms is Christo's: wrapping things up. What his work offers is not in any sense the classical aesthetic of the veil allowing forms to show through. The point, for him, is to make something disappear: an island, a cliff, a bridge, a

19. French television holds a 'telethon' event for muscular dystrophy sufferers and a similar annual event for people with AIDS.

monument, and hence to put it completely out of circulation. Allusively, of course, and for a limited time, but the phantasm is clearly to obliterate the object once and for all. The dream is that once the veil is removed, the hill (or the Reichstag) will really have disappeared, the way David Copperfield does these things (though what was 'aesthetic' illusion in Christo becomes pure illusionism with Copperfield). And, in the case of the Reichstag, the operation was in the highest degree revealing: by removing from view this emblem of the most dramatic period of twentieth-century history, Christo inadvertently revealed how that history had disappeared. That conjuring trick would have been impossible before the disappearance of the Berlin Wall (conversely, it is hard to imagine Christo wrapping up the Berlin Wall when it actually existed). Five million visitors came to celebrate this aesthetic laundering of history. An ambiguous collective jubilation: if Nazism thrived on the aestheticization of politics, our new democracy thrives on the aestheticization of the end of history.

Here again, behind these techniques of conjuring-away and obliteration, veiling and disappearance, the double phantasm consists either in disappearing from our own view or asking what becomes of the object when *it* disappears from view. Once again, as ever, the problem of the real. What are we in the absence of the object? What becomes of the object when we are no longer there? Does it become real again?

We have another example of this suspension, this withdrawal from circulation – for reasons of preserving the real and the original – in the Combes d'Arc cave.[20] This is a paleontological wonder that was closed to the public before it was ever

20. The Combes d'Arc cave, which has been widely compared with Lascaux and Altamira, was discovered on 24 December 1994 by Jean-Marie Chauvet at Vallon-Pont d'Arc in the Ardèche. Some time later, Mr Jean Clottes, the 'conservateur général du patrimoine', announced that the caves would be 'preserved for ever from the curiosity of the public'.

opened – in its way put under wraps – with its original paintings, sequestered for their own preservation, passing straight into a virtual existence from which they will not re-emerge. In this same spirit, a 'total nature reserve entirely off-limits to humans' has been created in the Écrins National Park.[21] In the absence of man, it is hoped that an original flora and fauna will be rediscovered there, a 'state of nature' within the space of a century! Increasingly, whole chunks of the biosphere will be buried in order to restore them to a state of artificial authenticity. They are being protected, deep-frozen, put under wraps, in the insane hope that our own traces can be erased and things can be restored to their initial, original state. For we know that with us and all our undertakings, the world will never be real or original again, and that everything is doomed, henceforth, to the curse of the screen, the curse of the simulacrum. We are in a world where the essential function of the sign is to make reality disappear and at the same time to mask that disappearance. Behind each image something has disappeared (it is not so much what it represents as this conjuring trick inherent in the image which gives it its force as sign). It is the same with the illusionism of information and memory. Behind every news item an event has disappeared; on the pretext of providing news and information, events are taken from us one by one. In this way, they enter the realm of the virtual, like the sealed-off wall paintings, like the buildings wrapped up by Christo – like the Chernobyl reactors sealed away in their concrete sarcophagi. In this way, the threat of a nuclear catastrophe has also passed into virtual reality. That was the greatest operation of 'putting an object under wraps' in history, costing somewhere between one and four billion dollars, and taking ten years to complete. The biggest object ever taken out of circulation for all time.

21. The Écrins national park, which lies in the area between Grenoble, Briançon and Gap, contains a central zone of 91,740 hectares in which there are no permanent inhabitants.

And should we add here the people of Strasbourg religiously burying a jumbled cocktail of signs of the human species (cassettes, an opera, a bra, etc.) in a container that is not intended to be opened until the year 3050? A provincial variant of the capsule sent into interstellar space some years ago with the noblest attestations to our humanity on board (some music by Bach, a photo of Liz Taylor, etc.). The oddest thing is that, at the same time as we are burying these signs of the present in the future (who are they intended for, if not for some other species than our own, for a world we shall have no further part in and which amounts therefore to an absolute origin?), where the traces of our own species and all the others are concerned, we are digging up everything that can be dug up. We desperately want nothing to have disappeared. And in some cases we are exhuming things that have been buried since the world began (the Lascaux caves) in order to put them immediately out of harm's way and keep them from view until the end of the world. What is the meaning of these things which will have hardly had time to pass through the stage of reality before being consigned to the status of video? Why wrench these traces, objects and vestiges from the secret lairs where they were alive, when they will immediately decompose in the open air? Conversely, what is the point of cryogenizing (like Disney in his liquid nitrogen capsule), freezing and museifying art works and cultures in order to afford them an improbable, artificial immortality, unless we have obscurely sensed that everything is disappearing? Even the human genome is declared part of the 'universal heritage'. Isn't this a way of sequestering it, as though it 'belonged to us', as though it were our biological capital? Isn't it also a way of putting it under wraps, of embalming it, as though we were aware that, having discovered it, we are capable now of destroying it?

Like the illusionist in the story, we are suddenly aware of the rapid, unintended disappearance of something very precious (a disappearance for which we must in some way be responsible). But of what? And how are we to bring it back?

'One should not believe that truth remains truth when you remove its veil,' said Nietzsche. But we should not believe either, as we seem to (we, who are contemporaries of the stripping-bare of the truth), that truth becomes truth again when we dress it once more and wrap it up. We should not believe that the real, which for us is dissipating into visibility and transparency, has a chance of becoming real again only if we make it disappear and render it invisible.

It is true that, to make something exist today, the best tactic is to play at making it disappear, to mask it so that it recovers the power of illusion. However, the revived object is never the same again. The real and nature, even revived, only get a secondary existence.

20 November 1995

Sexuality as a Sexually Transmitted Disease

Somewhere in New England, not far from Dartmouth College, you still find Shaker villages. In accordance with the religious law of that sect, the sexes live meticulously separate lives and do not reproduce (the world being given over to evil, there is no point perpetuating it; the only proper course is to await the Last Judgement). Now, on the nearby campus, which, like the other American campuses was one of the centres of sexual liberation, more or less the same situation pertains: the sexes no longer touch each other, no longer rub shoulders with each other, no longer attempt to seduce each other. Without any explicit prohibition or discrimination, they find themselves – in the name of sexual harassment and for obsessive fear of it – in the same condition of apartheid as prevails among the Shakers. The AIDS obsession doubtless plays a role in this voluntary exiling of sex – though there are never any causal relations in these kinds of things: AIDS is perhaps just one of the obscure pathways for a disaffection with sex which began long before the appearance and spread of that disease. It seems here that sexuality itself is at issue – each sex being, as it were, afflicted with a sexually transmitted disease that is sex itself.

There is a fear of catching AIDS, but a fear also of simply catching sex. There is a fear of catching anything whatever which might seem like a passion, a seduction, a responsibility. And, in this sense, it is once again the male who has most deeply fallen victim to the negative obsession with sex. To the point of withdrawing from the sexual game, exhausted by having to bear such a risk, and no doubt also wearied by having historically assumed the role of sexual power for so long. Of which feminism and female liberation have divested him, at least *de jure* (and, to a large extent, *de facto*). But things are more complicated than this, because the male who has been emasculated in this way and stripped of his power, has taken advantage of this situation to fade from the scene, to disappear – doffing the phallic mask of a power which has, in any event, become increasingly dangerous.

This is the paradoxical victory of the movement for feminine emancipation. That movement has succeeded too well and now leaves the female faced with the (more or less tactical and defensive) defaulting of the male. A strange situation ensues, in which women no longer protest against male power, but are resentful of the 'powerlessness' of the male. The defaulting of the male now fuels a deep dissatisfaction generated by disappointment with a sexual liberation which is going wrong for everyone. And this dissatisfaction finds expression, contradictorily, in the phantasm of sexual harassment. This is, then, a very different scenario from traditional feminism. Women are no longer alienated by men, but dispossessed of the masculine, dispossessed of the vital illusion of the other and hence also of their own illusion, their desire and privilege as women. It is this same effect which causes children secretly to hate their parents, who no longer wish to assume the role of parent and seize the opportunity of children's emancipation to liberate themselves as parents and relinquish their role. What we have, then, is no longer violence on the part of children in rebellion against the parental order, but hatred on the part of children dispossessed of their status and illusion as children. The person who liberates himself is never who you thought he was. This defaulting of the male has knock-on effects which extend into the biological order. Recent studies have found a fall in the rate of sperm in the seminal fluid, but, most importantly, a decline of their will to power: they no longer compete to go and fertilize the ovum. There is no competition any more. Are they, too, afraid of responsibility? Should we see this as a phenomenon analogous to what is going on in the visible sexual world, where a reticence to fulfil roles and a dissuasive terror exerted by the female sex currently prevail? Is this an unintended side-effect of the battle against harassment – the assault of sperm being the most elementary form of sexual harassment?

Despite appearances, this sexual disaffection and deterrence have nothing to do with any new prohibition of a religious or moral nature. All those prohibitions and inhibitions disappeared long ago. And the women who decorate the campuses with purple ribbons to mark rapes (in this way, every woman raped, or threatened with rape or dreaming of rape signals the memory of the crime publicly, in the same way as, in the USA, yellow ribbons signalled the memory of soldiers who had gone off to the Gulf War) – these women, representative of a new aggressive order and, simultaneously, of a new victim order – are certainly not victims of indecent exposure. There would seem, rather, to be a nostalgia for prohibitions in all this – or for anything that might resemble them – a reflex reaction to a virtual liberation of sexual mores and a banalization of sexuality now perceived as more dangerous than traditional censorship (which at least allowed transgression). A demand for a prohibition (for a rule, a limit, an obligation) which you can interpret as you will (and doubtless see as negative) from the psychological and political point of view – from the point of view of liberation and progress – but which may look like an instinctual defence of the species in respect of its sexual function, which is threatened by its emancipation and its very fulfilment.

Sexual harassment (the obsession with it and with AIDS) as a ruse of the species to revive the anxiety around sexuality – and more particularly a ruse on women's part to revive desire (men's desire, but their own too)? A very banal strategy (but a fatal one in the case of AIDS) to turn sex into something other than the sequence without consequence which it is becoming today, with all forms of sexual liberation – including contraception – moving ultimately in the direction of an 'erotic entropy' (Sloterdijk).

For what, in a traditional order, was accounted a liberation and a transgression (contraception) changes its meaning in a world moving increasingly towards asexual reproduction. Sexuality without reproduction leads on to reproduction without sexuality, and what was freedom of choice becomes quite simply the growing hold of the system over all forms of generation.

So, with the hatred that comes of disillusion following in the wake of liberatory violence, and the demand for prohibitions following in the wake of the problematic removal of all prohibitions, a kind of sentimental, familial, political and moral revisionism has ensued and is currently winning out on all fronts. This tidal wave of revisionism, running counter to all the liberations of the twentieth century, finds expression also in repentance and the decline of sex. Whereas in the past it was freedom, desire, pleasure and love which seemed to be sexually transmitted, today it seems to be hatred, disillusionment, distrust and resentment between the sexes. Behind this polemic over harassment lies a later form of Marcuse's 'repressive desublimation' – the lifting of prohibitions and repressions ushering in a new system of suppressions and control. In our view, this might better be described as a 'depressive resublimation', leading directly to moral, if not indeed religious, fundamentalism, or, at any rate, beneath the fantasies of rape and harassment, to a sexual protectionism. In that protectionism, sex, for the male, becomes the obsession with a lost function, which now finds an outlet only in fantasies of rape; for the female, it becomes an instrument of blackmail. We are living through all this, subjectively and collectively: a painful phase transition after what was perhaps merely an illusion of progress and liberation. But we have no idea whatever as to the ultimate designs of the species here (nor even if it has any). Animal species react to situations of crisis, shortage or overpopulation with sexual continence and automatic sterility. We are perhaps reacting similarly – quite outside any subjective conviction or ideology – to a situation of plenty, liberation, well-being and *release* which, being quite alien to the species over its history, we find agonizing and inhuman. The hatred which the issue of sexual harassment releases may perhaps simply be the repentance of a liberty, individuality and freedom to express our desire which were hard won, and which we are now paying for with a new-found voluntary servitude. Might not servitude itself become a sexually transmitted disease?

4 December 1995

Sovereignty of the Strike

It is difficult to speak of this strike in terms which are not tritely political or economic – this behaviour which is both banal and demented, this silent solidarity, this quasi-joyful, excessive commitment of the strikers and others to a destiny that has already been sacrificed, come what may.[22] We can undoubtedly see in it a form of radical questioning of the fact of being governed (the fact of being exploited already being part of an old history). But, as with all good questions, there is no answer to this one, for governments will never have an answer to the questions: Why do you govern us? Why do you speak in our name? Why do you want to do good to us?

It has not been easy, over the generations, to push people into work, school, health and security – into the economy of their own lives. It has always been the understanding that the masses did not know what they wanted and that you had to will and act for them. That has even been the sign of a courageous democracy:

22. The reference is to the French strike wave of December 1995, aimed at preventing the implementation of public spending cuts associated with the adoption of the Maastricht Treaty.

doing the popular good against the people's will. So, they have been evangelized in the name of Enlightenment and, like it or not, they have allowed it to happen, have let it be done to them. They are rebelling today against this forced evangelization. Or rather they are anticipating their own disappearance (for all these social categories – railwaymen, civil servants, craftsmen – are destined to disappear in any event, like workers and peasants), but doing so in a joyful way, or at any rate in a way that is invigorating and exuberant. Active self-destruction can be preferable to slow extermination. And this suicide is the more forceful for showing up for all to see the inanity of governments which are incapable of any response whatever, and merely rely on inertia and decay to do the work for them. The key element in this unconscious strategy of the masses is to disqualify governments by exposing them – either for their violence and oppression as in 1968, or for their transparency and indigence as today. In 1968 it was the *auto-da-fé* of a bourgeois, elitist, academic culture joyfully doing away with its privileges, destroying its consecrated places, sensing what was inevitably to come: the demagogy of a mass culture to be unleashed on us over the next twenty years. Something rather similar is happening now with all kinds of disappearing occupational categories: they are playing out their anachronistic resurrection (and this includes the trade unions) in a last stand which does at least transform this exit from History into an event. So, there are movements which lag behind their own history, but are ahead of the history being foisted on them.

Why do you expect people to sacrifice the current social security regime, which they have themselves, as it happens, pushed to the brink of catastrophe? If they are not to be recognized as citizens, it is their only means of blackmailing the State, their only way of extorting money from it. The result is to show up the State (and the whole of the political class) as being, by its *de facto* impotence, even further down the road to disappearance than those who call on its aid. 'Ask not what the State can do for you; ask what you can do for the State' (to borrow a famous phrase). For it can do nothing – nothing economically and certainly nothing politically, being at the whim of markets and capital flows which are way beyond its control. Do not even ask the State what it can do for the State: it has made itself redundant.

But the strike movement is not content merely to relegate the state to the passenger seat. It is practically testing out a different way of living, a social condition which could function at a minimum level of operation, capable of deploying a fantastic energy in the absence of the State or a system of control. These people setting out for their workplaces at four in the morning, these people fired with an ambulatory – if not indeed jubilatory – rage. Of course, they are afraid of losing their jobs, but at the same time they are setting out their stalls. They are proving that they can get by on their own, that they can cope without institutional mechanisms and powers. For a moment, at least, they will have proved this. This is what the strike in action represents: the welling-up of an incredible capacity to construct your life in total freedom, to do without all those who want at all costs to do good *to you*. Such a demonstration has a lethal effect on any kind of power. Its arrogance is met with a collective upsurge of pride, even if this takes the form of a pig-headed defence of those on the scrap heap or a sectional defence of the 'economically under-developed'. It is the very excess of the strike and its spilling-over in time, its exceeding of its own objectives, which expresses – beyond any economic stakes involved – what is symbolically at issue at a deep level in this strike. The surest sign of this sovereignty of the strike – and a lethal sign for governments – is that, when governments no longer respect people, people begin to respect each other.

Walking, walking – this has been the great revelation of this strike movement. Much more than traditional demonstrations. For in social fracture, circulation is the crux. The only circulation in this society is the circulation of elites and networks, the circulation of money and information in real time. An abstract circulation, in-accessible to most people. It is against this that people are walking. They are walking in the deferred[23] time of space against the real time of the networks – in the physical time of the journey against the breakneck circulation of flows. It is an orig-inal and direct form of protest against the very norm of this society. The contrast with the Telethon, which happened coincidentally to be held during the period of the strike, was stunning. There too you saw people walking, running and cycling out of a sense of media solidarity to keep the Telethon going – with its records in millions of kilometres, its displays in millions of francs. And the contrast with the strike showed up just where the Society of the Spectacle had taken refuge: in the servile organization of charity.

You have to have (by some miracle) caught an empty TGV train – the last one from Lyon to Paris – without tickets, without inspectors, perhaps even without a driver (the phantom train of the strike) to appreciate the incredible ease of our tech-nical automatisms and, at the same time, the magical possibility of a removal of all controls – the whole of society reflecting the current situation by functioning at a minimum level of operation. An immense relief (in Italy, the back-up services already function better than the normal ones). What this long march of a society also expresses is the dream of a lightened society, a society in which democracy is no longer the condescending democracy of elites or the democracy of helots clam-ouring for advancement, but one in which people would advance under their own constraints and by their own laws.

23. '*Différé*'. In French, the term *en différé* refers to a 'pre-recorded' television broadcast. French television commonly shows events – particularly sporting events – in an 'as-live' format. That is to say, they are recorded, but broadcast in their entirety rather than in the form of highlights. Hence the contrast here with 'real time'.

The 1992 referendum on Europe was the first indication of a 'democratic' coalition of all powers – political, media, cultural and intellectual – against a recalcitrant public opinion resistant to the universal gospel of rationality. It is now clear that two antagonistic forces are in opposition, and there is nothing to suggest that they can be reconciled. This is not just a social, but a mental fracture. Between a manifest power which believes it is moving in the direction of history (even if, in the end, that history of the cybernetic and technocratic domestication of the world makes no more sense to it than to others) and an irreducible opposing power which is growing day by day: not the power of intelligence, but the power of cunning – of the ruse of the victims of history, of the cunning, ironic movement of the masses; a power which runs parallel to history and is opposed at any price to a single order, an enforced orthodoxy of thought, a single currency and the stereotyped language of the universal. Two antagonistic forces no longer of the order of the class struggle: the one, the rational power, with a (decreasing) mastery of signs and language, and an (increasing) mastery of the techniques of persuasion and discussion. The other fragmentary, erratic and non-representative; the force on which the linear sense of progress and history has been imposed. No one wants to acknowledge that force. For no one understands the subterranean preparatives to anger.

There are events, said Nietzsche, which take a century to reach us, truths we do not dare face up to which remain stuck in a kind of purgatory. One such truth, no doubt, is that events no longer take place now with the tide of history and political strategies, but against history and against politics. If we are being offered the New European Order, dovetailing into the New World Order, as the key occurrence of this century's end, then our French strike, with its millions of walkers and millions standing silently by in solidarity is indeed the anti-event, the counter-event par excellence.

18 December 1995

Tierra del Fuego – New York

Land of disasters, as has been said. Devastated forests seemingly felled by some recent cataclysm. Hulks of wrecked ships. Graveyards of immigrants (why so many Yugoslavs?) and sailors. But there is another disaster here today, the disaster of a completely anachronistic modernity – a chaotic, incoherent cowboy-film modernity: concrete, dust, duty-free, transistors, petrol, computers and the hubbub of useless traffic – as though the silence of the ends of the earth had to be obliterated. All that is inhuman here is sublime in its natural desolation. All that is human is sordid: civilization's wastes.

There is some justice in the fact that modern man actually treats himself as a waste product, having previously treated the Indians that way. A higher justice, which balances out the destinies of persecutor and victim. Those closest to these Fuegian Indians (and we know neither their names nor what crime they committed to be wiped out as they were) are the outcasts, the criminals, the inmates of the old Ushuaia jailhouse, whose photos adorn the museum.[24] This one in particular,

24. The Museo Maritimo de Ushuaia is located in the old prison building.

of whom a superb photo remains, though we do not know his name, his crime, his ultimate destiny or the date of his death – the photo of the perfect unknown prisoner. Or the photo of Radowitzski, the anarchist who blew up the Buenos Aires police chief (the renowned Falcon), broke out of jail, was recaptured, attempted suicide, was pardoned after twenty years and ended his days in exile.

Ranged against these criminals and Indians, the Salesian missionaries – charitable parasites of this ill-starred land, which they evangelize like the lichen that wraps itself around the forests of nothofagus and submerges those trees as they are gobbled up by it.

On every side is nothingness, wasteland, sterile horizons, infinite vistas. There is, in fact, neither nature nor culture here, but a savage denial of both – a denial of landscape in the nothingness of the wind, the sooty sky, the Bahía Inútil; a denial of culture in the nothingness of the towns (but how else could it have been once those who ended up in their own language calling themselves 'the foreigners' had been exterminated?). The geographical remoteness highlights the contrast between the two without giving any meaning – even a surrealistic one – to their being huddled together like this. What you discover here is not a new, original world, but the relentless mix of a wild, elemental form and an equally relentlessly destructive grip exerted by the human race.

The phantasm of the ends of the earth. You think you have left the world behind and cut the umbilical cord. Not a bit of it. The other world is already there well before you are, with its 'real time' – in this unreal, timeless land. You can receive a fax of an article that appeared in Paris only this morning. There is, then, no end of the world. Or everywhere is at the ends of the earth. Wherever we are, we are, at the same time, at the extreme outer reaches. One becomes, oneself, an extreme phenomenon – beyond one's own end. Now, the phantasm of the ends of the earth is a phantasm of the territory having some extreme furthest point – the symbol of a possible end and of the outer reaches of thought. It is a fantasy of verifying that, despite what they say, the earth is not a sphere and does not have that hope-sapping curvature.

The Alakaluf did not know they were at the ends of the earth. They were where they were and nowhere else – something we shall never be. For the sailors, adventurers and missionaries, it wasn't the end either: they discovered a world entirely unlike their own, but one against which they could pit themselves, a new frontier. We arrive here today with only an imaginary notion of the ends of the earth (to which space travel long since put an end). And while the Fuegians were never parted from their fires (they carried them everywhere, even on their boats in the form of burning embers), we take pains to carry our artificial coldness with us everywhere – even into glacial latitudes.

After Tierra del Fuego, New York. After the ends of the earth, the centre of the earth. A double extremity: the point where the curvature of the earth comes to an end; the place where human technology and verticality have gone as far as they can go. But each gives the impression of being on another planet. The archaeological stillness of time on Tierra del Fuego, its depth. And here in New York its superficial acceleration. The two are equally timeless. And if, down in the Southern hemisphere, the sun lies to the north at noon (which always seems so marvellous to a Westerner), it seems just as strange that the same sun rises and sets on New York, whose astral theme seems so indifferent to any other orbit but its own.

When you are at the tip of Manhattan, by Battery Park and the Staten Island ferry, you might think you were at the furthest point of Tierra del Fuego, on the banks of the Beagle Channel. On a New York morning, you have the same impression of primordial energy, of a primal scene, as at a dawning of the world. Everywhere else, the energy expended gives an impression of wear and fatigue, of being consumed by the activity. Here, by contrast, it regenerates in hyperactivity.

Only natural energies give this impression of inexhaustibility. Here it is the artificial energy, the high voltage, which gives New York this quality of a perpetual anticyclone.

Primal scene, primitive society – perhaps. But when you go directly from Patagonia to Broadway and Times Square, you cannot but be terrified by the proliferation of the human race. You feel like Ishi, the last Indian, wrenched by the anthropologist from the solitude of his race and hurled into the crowds of San Francisco. In his bewilderment at the number of simultaneously present human beings (he had never before seen more than thirty or forty together), the only explanation he could find was that all the dead were present alongside the living, since it was unthinkable that the gods could watch over so many existences at once. Ten dead people for every living one seems a good proportion. As in the primal forest of Tierra del Fuego for example, where there is one living tree to every ten dead ones. Hence the conclusion that, in the thronging metropolises, nine out of ten human beings are living dead, are zombies. Their physical appearance is deceptive, for the so-called human beings who no longer have any physical contact other than through crowds and no human relations other than through communications are truly virtual corpses or ghosts. Only a few hundred or a few thousand perhaps maintain a secret bond, the only living symbolic chain in this immense, incapacitated human genome.

The millions of people in the streets seem to have nothing to do but be at the centre of the world and head off in all directions, in a dispersal as spectacular as it is useless. Nothing else to do but make New York exist in its useless, eccentric form. A city of the utmost urgency, a once-and-for-all city with no tomorrow – very far removed from any democratic form of representation. In New York the people represent only themselves, not the rest of society. The city represents only itself, not the rest of America. This is what gives it its global importance. It is a detector, a sensor of prestige; its charm is to have transformed not only the rest of the United States, but the rest of the world into an immense province (which in no way detracts from the charm of the provinces).

There is no social bond here, no conviviality, no collective sentimentality, no responsibility towards past or future. You don't reproduce in New York. It isn't a city made for reproducing. Yet everything happens here. Hence the foreboding of catastrophe which hovers over the whole city – though it is an upbeat sense of foreboding. Down in Tierra del Fuego, at the edges of the earth, in the lonely Antarctic wastes, there is a poignant sense of natural catastrophe, which reaches back to time immemorial, and of genocide which dates from recent history. A world devastated by wind, ice, human predators, the exhaustion of earlier ages – a disaster continuing even now. A curse which the Fuegians maintained with their own gods, when they had any (it is difficult for the gods to find a foothold in a pitiless world, to embody elemental powers which are themselves pitiless to one another).

The sense of catastrophe you get in New York is quite different. It is the sense of a vital catastrophe, of what can end only in excess and prodigality. The maximum imminence of present time and hence the exhaustion of any future, of any future energy, which is gathered into a single instant, an absolute present.

Having said this, we no doubt have a naive view of energy. An entropic view. Whereas energy – the millennial energy of the wind in Patagonia or the energy of humanity's workings – is doubtless inexhaustible.

1 January 1996

World Debt and Parallel Universe

The electronic display of the American national debt in Times Square registers an astronomical figure of some thousands of billions of dollars, increasing at the staggering rate of 20,000 dollars a second. The electronic display at Beaubourg registers the millions of seconds separating us from the year 2000. The one, representing time, falls steadily. The other, representing money, rises vertiginously. One is a countdown to zero second. The other, by contrast, tends towards infinity. Both imply catastrophe, at least in the imaginary register. In the Beaubourg case, the catastrophe of the exhaustion of time; in the American case, the catastrophe of the debt beginning to grow exponentially, bringing a world financial crash in its wake.

In fact, this debt will never be paid off. No debt will ever be paid off. The final accounting will never take place. If our days are numbered, accounted for, the absent capital, for its part, is beyond any accounting. If the United States is already in virtual breach of its obligations, this will have no effects. There will be no Judgement Day for this virtual bankruptcy. One has merely to enter the exponential or virtual mode to be released from all responsibility, since there is no longer any reference, any referential world to serve as measure.

This disappearance of the referential universe is an entirely new situation. When you contemplate the electronic display on Broadway, you have the impression of something taking off into the stratosphere; the debt figure might be the distance, expressed in light years, of a galaxy moving away from us in the cosmos, the escape velocity of a terrestrial satellite. And, indeed, it is a satellite: the debt moves on an orbit that is entirely its own, the orbit of capital released from any economic contingency, moving in a parallel universe, having escaped, by its very acceleration, from any relapse into the banal universe of production, value and use. Not even an orbital universe, but an exorbital, ex-centred, eccentric one. And the probability of its ever re-entering our world is faint indeed.

This is why, from this point on, no debt will be paid off. It can at best be bought back at a knock-down price and put back on to a debt market – the public sector borrowing requirement, the national debt, the world debt – having once again become an exchange value. It is unlikely the debt will ever be called in, and this is what gives it its incalculable value. For, suspended as it is in this way, it is our only insurance against time. Unlike the countdown, which signifies the exhaustion of time, the indefinitely deferred debt is our guarantee that time itself is inexhaustible. Now, we very much need assuring about time in this way at the very point when the future itself is tending to be wholly consumed in real time. Clearing the debt, balancing up the books, writing off Third World debt – these are things not even to be contemplated. It is only the disequilibrium of the debt, its proliferation, its promise of infinity, which keeps us going. The global, planetary debt clearly has no meaning in traditional terms of obligation and credit. On the other hand, it is our true collective claim on each other – a symbolic claim, by which persons, companies and nations find themselves bound to one another through lack. Each is bound to the other (even the banks) by their virtual bankruptcy, as accomplices are bound by their crime. All assured of existing for each other in the shade of a debt which cannot be settled or written off, since the repayment of the accumulated world debt would take far more than the funds available. The only sense of it, then, is to bind all civilized human beings into the same destiny as creditors. Just as nuclear weapons, stockpiled across the world to a point of considerable planetary overkill, have no other meaning than to bind all human beings into a single destiny of threat and deterrence.

One understands, then, why the Americans make such a show of their debt. The initiative is supposed to shame the State for its bad management and alert the citizens to an imminent collapse of the finances and public services. But the exorbitant scale of the figures robs them of all meaning. It is, in fact, just a massive advertising exercise and, indeed, the luminous billboard looks for all the world like a triumphant stock market index that has broken all records. The population contemplate it with the fascination they might accord to a world record (though few gather in front of the Beaubourg digital clock to see the run-in to the end of the century). At the same time, the people are collectively in the same situation as the Tupolev test pilot who right up to the last second could see his aircraft nose dive and crash into the ground on his internal video circuit. Did he, by some last-minute reflex, glance at the image as he died? He could have imagined himself living out his last moments in virtual reality. Did the image survive the man if only for a fraction of a second? Or was it the other way about? Does virtual reality survive the real world's catastrophic end?

Our real artificial satellites are the world debt, the speculative capital and the nuclear warheads which girdle the earth on their orbital round. Having become pure artefacts – sidereally mobile and instantly convertible – they have at last found their true place, more extraordinary than the Stock Exchange, the banks and the silos: the orbit on which they rise and set like artificial suns.

The latest of these exponentially growing parallel universes is the world of the Internet and the global information systems. Here too, the irresistible growth, the outgrowth of information, could be posted up in real time in terms of millions of in-dividuals and millions of operations – that information now so extensive that it no longer has any connection with the acquisition of knowledge. As of now, we can say that this immense potential will never be redeemed, in the sense of a use or purpose ever being found for it. Things here, then, are exactly as they are with debt: *information is as inexpiable as debt*, in the sense that we shall never be able to settle our account with it. Moreover, the storage of data, the accumulation and worldwide circulation of information, in every respect resemble the build-up of an irremissible debt. And, here again, as soon as this proliferating information far exceeds the needs and capaci-ties of the individual and the species in general, it has no other meaning than to bind all humanity in a single destiny of cerebral automatism and mental underdevelopment. For it is clear that, though a certain dose of information reduces our ignorance, a mas-sive dose of artificial intelligence can only convince us of the failings of our natural intelligence and plunge us deeper into them. The worst thing in a human being is to know too much and not to be equal to one's knowledge. It is the same with respon-sibility and emotional capacity: the media, by perpetually assailing us with violence, misfortune and catastrophe, far from firing some kind of collective solidarity, merely demonstrate our real impotence and plunge us into panic and remorse.

All these parallel universes, caught in an autonomous, exponential logic, are time bombs. This is clear with nuclear power, but it is the case too with debt and speculative capital. The tiniest irruption of these worlds into our own, the merest intersection of their orbit with ours would immediately smash the fragile equilib-rium of our trade and our economies. It would (or will) be the same with the total liberation of information, making us free radicals desperately seeking their mol-ecules in a rarefied cyberspace.

Reason would doubtless dictate that we reintegrate these worlds into ours, into an homogeneous universe: that a peaceful use be found for nuclear power, that all debts be paid off, that speculative capital be reinvested in social wealth, and that the whole of information become part of knowledge. But this is no doubt a dangerous utopia. It would be better for these universes to remain parallel and for their suspended threat, their eccentricity, to protect us. Parallel and eccentric as they are, they are nonetheless ours. We created them like this, beyond our reach, as an ersatz transcendence; we put them into orbit as a kind of catastrophic imaginary. But perhaps this is all to the good. For, if the cohesion of our societies was in the past maintained by the 'imaginary' of progress, it is maintained today by the 'imaginary' of catastrophe.

15 January 1996

The Shadow of the Commendatore

It has been an extraordinary adventure, this cancer of Mitterand's. After being concealed, hidden and repressed for fifteen years, it was 'illegally' revealed by Dr. Gubler in *Le Grand Secret* – at which point the courts intervened with a ban.[25] It was then revived on the Internet in virtual space, and, in the end, placed virtually under lock and key in the person of the offending cybercafé

25. The book *Le Grand Secret* by Claude Gubler (Mitterand's personal physician) and Michel Gonod was published by Plon on 17 January 1996, nine days after the president's death. It claimed that Mitterand's prostate cancer was first diagnosed in 1981 and that medical information after that date was falsified at the president's request. Gubler also argued that, by the end of his second term, the president was so ill he could barely fulfil his duties. The book was banned on 18 January when the Mitterand family brought an action against the publishers and Dr. Gubler (for breach of confidentiality). By that date, 33,000 copies are said to have been sold. The ban was confirmed in the Paris Appeal Court on 13 March 1996. The text of the book has since been available periodically on the Internet.

owner.[26] From one cancer to another. From cancer of the prostate to the cancer of information. Since the biological secondaries cannot be spirited away by medicine, they are spirited away by silence. Since the secondary cancers of information cannot be spirited away, they are prohibited by law. This elegantly resolves the problems of data protection and bioethics, of openness and unchecked proliferation: use the law to stop the viruses. Sadly, the secondaries have already got out into the outside world – through the 'mirror sites'.

Having passed through all the phases of secrecy and openness in this way, Mitterand's cancer can be seen as emblematic of his reign, based on the systematic usage of secrecy and, particularly towards the end, on the calculated trickling-out of the parts of his life he found too shameful to mention. His cancer can be seen on these two levels, as having crowned a life which might be said to have begun with the assassination attempt on the avenue de l'Observatoire.[27] Simulated attack, dissimulated cancer – in both cases, he escapes by a minor miracle (he leapfrogs the railings; he leapfrogs a death foretold), then arranges for the facts to come out, without anyone being able to make them count. All the lies of his life were given

26. The text was apparently first placed on the Internet by Pascal Barbraud, manager of the 'Le Web' cybercafé in Besançon (Doubs). On 26 January 1996, Barbraud was arrested by the Besançon police, not for any infringement of the ban on publication, but because of a three-month sentence passed on him on 20 September 1994 at Nanterre for desertion of his family and non-payment of alimony. In the meantime, the text of Gubler's book had appeared on a variety of mirror sites from which it could be downloaded. On 5 February 1996, the equipment at his cybercafé was seized as a result of action taken by one of Barbraud's creditors.

27. In October 1959 Mitterand's car apparently came under machine-gun fire on the avenue de l'Observatoire. He escaped by jumping over railings (or in some accounts, over a hedge) into the grounds of the Observatory. Mitterand was subsequently accused by various far Right personalities of having staged the attack himself for his own political ends.

to the French people, which was made to swallow them. Not only did he cultivate insider-trading, where his illness and many other things were concerned – everyone in power does that – but he cultivated the opposite: blackmail by threat of revelation, a coded revelation so to speak, more or less orchestrated in secret by himself (his extreme-Rightist past, Bousquet, the Elysée scandals, his second sex life, his clandestine daughter, his retrospective cancer), which he used as a grim form of advertising.

He delighted in having the public swallow the fraud and cunning of what has been the greatest case of embezzlement in recent history: the embezzlement of the socialist heritage for ends which were impenetrable, though they were certainly not social (nor perhaps historic: the appetite for glory or historical concupiscence were not uppermost with him, as they were with De Gaulle, but rather sarcasm, the Commendatore's rigid manipulation, the obscure, dominating irony of the person in the 'place du mort', which the stiff mask of a face and uncertain, pale smile already expressed to perfection). But, above all, the intercepting of opinion,[28] the political de-vitalization of a society into which he can be said to have instilled, for years, the imagining of his own death.

And to have thrown down a kind of challenge to servility in doing this – a challenge to the servility of the masses (though, once again, this is part of ordinary governance) and the servility of those around him, for whom, one fondly imagines, he felt a 'lordly' contempt. At least you want this to be the case, since he had so many contemptible people around him! To the point where, in repaying his contempt, one is merely doing him homage and remaining faithful to his memory. For the power of contempt alone drove him. And that, paradoxically, deserves respect.

28. 'La captation de l'opinion'. Captation has overtones both of telephone tapping and the improper solicitation of a legacy.

In the end, history will have proved him right, since the people – the dear old people – flattered, deceived and made to look retrospectively ridiculous by all that has been hidden from them (worse: by all that was revealed to them too late, always too late, and then impudently hushed up and whitewashed afterwards) will have compliantly wept collectively over his death (we shall not even speak of the sadness of the courtiers and the *pentiti*).

This might even be said to be the most demoralizing thing in the whole story. For in the end Mitterand himself has no case to answer. All he can be accused of is the servility of other people, the extraordinary indulgence, complicity and wilful lack of lucidity he promoted and the fruits of which he enjoyed throughout his reign: this collective failure of the political reflex, this growing impotence in the face of the enormous insider-deal government had become. We may, for the time being, mourn Mitterand (since, in any event, he has organized the mourning himself – perhaps he even ordered his *cliché mortuaire* and its distribution, this is all part of the same logic), but what we are going to have to mourn forever, given this gloomy consensus around his death, including around the virtual corpse he had been for fifteen years, is any prospect of democracy, any chance of any sort of understanding and openness in public affairs. The point is proven: nothing can ever change. He brought that home to us; that was his victory, and I am sure he will have delighted in that bitter truth even from beyond the grave.

It must be said that he sacrificed himself – even in death – to the hypostasis of his own person. The ambition and arrogance of 'great men' and the automatic servility of the masses are, in our media system, mere extensions of each other. Unless voluntary servitude, far from being a capitulation, is actually a double-edged sword and the people, which gets cannibalized, also cannibalizes the politicians. It is cannibalizing Mitterand – through all the posthumous revelations and the great popular show they make – with a necrophagous zeal equal to the therapeutic zeal he can be seen to have deployed to defer his own death. And that death, deferred over at least ten years, remains a mystery. Where did he get the energy from? It could only have been from the power of secrecy, and, more importantly, from the force which comes from the exercise of power, by a process of absorbing the energy of all those around him – feeding on that and regenerating from it, and leaving his entourage limp and subservient. The system is a simple one: take all the positive energies from the others; dump all the negative energy on them.

Adduction of positive flows, abduction of negative flows. Mitterand practised this strategy not just on the political class, but on the whole of French society. On the political society: liquidating the Communist Party, anaesthetizing the Right, vampirizing and parasiting a Socialist Party which he kept alive on a drip, though it was already in an advanced vegetative state (the political class's loss of its ability to reason – its going to pieces – was most clearly revealed in the suicide of Pierre Bérégovoy) and promoting a phoney Europe which he will hand on like a hot potato to all who follow him (second negative event of the reign: the referendum on Europe). On French society: it was by concealing his cancer that he managed to govern, but it was by projecting that cancer on to French society that he managed to survive for so long. Only by passing his secondary infections on to us during his reign and sucking the lifeblood one by one from those forces which could oppose that reign was he able to hold on for such a time. We were governed by a man solely preoccupied with his own death and dripping it in homeopathic doses into all the systems and tissues of political life – heading off any other way of imagining governance. For if, contrary to what is said of it, imagination has never dreamed of taking power, power has always dreamed of devouring the imagination – and has generally ended up devouring its own image.

This is why we should thank Mitterand for this personal obsession, since, by force of negativity, he can be said to have given us a remarkable political lesson. He has taught us that one could govern – that one could govern only – by virtue of an internal weakness, an anticipated death – but in secrecy and to the people's disgrace. For the people has indeed been disgraced, disgraced the way the last of the courtiers were. And this is very much the worst of it all. The people of France – to whom he passed on corruption on the sly, like a dirty picture slipped to them under the counter – were clearly made aware that they did not count for much.

This is the art of government today: government by negative means, by deterrence, by convincing people of their powerlessness. So it is still for them – for the betrayed, the insulted, those on the scrap heap, those who have been given the runaround – to take the shame of it all, and, indeed, to accept and absolve this state of affairs as something criminal but inevitable.

This is the abominable political lesson he can be said to have taught us. But, if his was merely the dead man's hand, who was steering the ship of state? Who but death itself?

5 February 1996

The Mirror of Corruption

A bill to reform the law on the misuse of public funds, amounting virtually to a veiled amnesty, almost made it to Parliament recently. And, make no mistake about it, it will come before it one day in some form or another. The Pelat affair has already been shelved.[29] What is euphemistically called the misuse of public funds often relates to the apportionment of funds and property that are almost as illicit as drugs money. You cannot, in fact, see where the chain of corruption begins and ends. Tapie embezzling money to fix football matches can be called corrupt, but isn't the Crédit Lyonnais, which so generously kept Tapie's coffers topped up, just as corrupt? (and indeed Tapie wasn't slow to criticize it in an effort to excuse his own actions). And doesn't all the money squandered in risky

29. Mr Patrice Pelat was said to have benefited from building work which was invoiced as part of projects relating to a hospital in Le Mans and a school at Courbevoie, but actually carried out on his property in Sologne. This was, allegedly, part of an arrangement to pay Mr Pelat back for obtaining a contract in North Korea. Mr Pelat was a friend of the French president François Mitterand and was in fact the man alleged by *Le Canard enchaîné* to have supplied Pierre Bérégovoy with the interest-free loan of 1 million francs in 1986. See note 11, p. 71

ventures by the same Crédit Lyonnais, like many other banks and financial in-stitutions, amount to embezzlement and misuse of public funds? No one speaks out against this scandal, on the grounds that it is not a matter for the law. But we know that there is much more 'legal' fraud than illegal. This throws the anti-corruption operation into perspective, and in a sense renders it ridiculous – that operation which, in its way, provides a cover for (and a diversion from) the real corruption.

Getting to the roots of corruption would be an endless business. No one could plumb its depths. Without any doubt, it is consubstantial with social functioning. But at least the 'war on corruption' evokes its spectre and presents us with it as spectacle. Now, the spectacle of corruption is a vital function in a democracy: it provides entertainment and has an educative, cathartic function. It does not produce any deep-seated bitterness; otherwise revolt would be permanently festering. In the end, corruption does not arouse any collective indignation (though, this, naturally, is filtered by the media). And, though it is positively an outrage, the amnesty bill which is in the offing (echoing the amnesty French members of parliament have generously granted themselves) – an amnesty which amounts virtually to an invi-tation to corruption – has not brought the outcry one would have expected from a body of democratic public opinion.

This is because, at bottom, no one believes in democracy. Everyone dimly real-izes that any system functions in denial of its own principles, transgressing its own rules. And this resignation over principles feeds an abashed consensus on the hidden, immoral rules by which our society operates. Corruption in democracy is simply the new form assumed by privilege – the rule in earlier societies – which has merely become illegal, thus adding further to its charm.

Corruption itself is, in this way, a vital function: a secret mechanism of a whole society, a source of political energy, a public service.

Everything in the ARC story is scandalous and repulsive, but is it not also scandalous that millions of people are prepared to give when asked to do so in any way by charities or the media?[30] How can we demand that officers of charities make rational and honest use of funds gathered so easily, and given so trustingly to such a shady charity? It would be amazing if they did so. Moreover, the skulduggery does not prevent the mystified victims from continuing to give with the same naivety. Isn't there an element of responsibility in this servility, whether spontaneous or orchestrated? What people ultimately want is to be given a chance to give, as they have elsewhere been given the chance to vote or, on any of the confessional TV programmes, the chance to speak. So those who satisfy this desire, taking their cut from it as they do, are performing a genuine public service. At any rate, the money misappropriated in the process, being deflected first from its useful (private) purposes, then from its useful (public) purposes by the cancer crooks, still meets the same fate: it is squandered. In this respect it is similar to the money sacrificed in gambling and in playing the lottery.

The State has not been alone in exploiting this formula in all the various forms of gambling. Are the improbable sums wasted on gambling for pointless (and hence immoral) purposes so different from the sums misappropriated by banks or companies to pay to politicians or embezzled by the bureaucrats of cancer research for purposes of lavish entertainment and advertising? The citizen is not punished for this 'misuse of private funds', for this immoral use of his own money. It might be said that the State encourages lotteries for the profit it makes from them. But you

30. Jacques Crozemarie, former president of ARC (Association de Recherche contre le Cancer), was found guilty of embezzling the charity's funds and sentenced to four years in prison by the Paris Court of Appeal. He was also fined 2.5 million francs and required to pay 200 million francs in damages to ARC.

could also say that the colossal reverses suffered by banking concerns through fraudulent property dealings have created thousands of jobs along the way: and is this not the number one priority?

In fact, interest and utility are never the key to the story. It has never been the primordial function of a society to put money and resources to moral ends, even if it is the alleged ideal of all our democracies. Money remains at all times and in all places the accursed share, the immoral share, the evil portion. And the primordial function remains that of managing that accursed share, of voiding and laundering money through gambling, waste, misappropriation and corruption; destroying money by its immoral use; destroying evil with evil. This is the strategy of evil, the politics of evil which preserves the symbolic equilibrium of a society. Evil be to him who evil thinks. No more than it is conceivable to rebalance debt (on the lines of the same ideal vision of credit and the proper use of money) is it conceivable that there will be an 'economically correct' social distribution of misspent money. That money, like debt, cannot be redeemed or transferred to a 'social satisfaction' of needs, for – and this is true of the most archaic or the most modern societies – every social bond is fundamentally threatened by money. The only solution, then, is to 'launder' it and, to that end, to misspend it, or at all costs to put it into circulation, as quickly as possible – to put the accursed share into orbit. Which is done, in their own tiny way, by individuals and, on a much larger scale, by all the syndicates of fraudsters.

Apart from being impractical, as experience has shown, the rational redistribution of resources is a dangerous ideology. It confuses means and ends. It believes that money is a means and can be redeemed by useful ends. A touching illusion. Money is a medium, not a means, and it has all the power of a medium which develops according to its own ends. 'Enlightened' minds think money, like man for Rousseau, would be naturally good if it were not misdirected toward evil. But the opposite is true: money is, by its very principle, of the order of evil; it is its destiny to work for evil and for it to move towards good it has to be subtly re-routed. Things here are as they are with human beings, whose fundamental passion, according to Freud, is and remains hatred. It is hatred which binds human beings together much more strongly than love. And it changes into love only by travelling down exceptional pathways, which remain forever fragile. This error on the part of people 'of good will' is fatal in the political management of societies, since it merely perpetuates evil by misunderstanding its guiding principle and the perverse economy on which our society is based.

If we follow the paths of this politics of evil, the ironic paths of corruption, we arrive at a reassuring conclusion: the fact is that corruption is the 'bad' which preserves us from the worst. Take the scandal which has been most in the headlines: the embezzlement of public or private funds for financing election campaigns or political parties. What finer end-goal for money than to be squandered in that supremely useless operation, that laughable venture, an election? These funds have at least genuinely vanished into thin air. It is merely corrupt money re-used for corrupt ends and at bottom that does little harm to the community. When you think what would have come of a healthy, enlightened management of these funds, all the projects for the public good which would have been visited upon us, all the gyratory road schemes, the thousands of useless offices – that whole superstructure, that urban, cultural blight, on which towns and even the smallest villages nowadays pride themselves! Not counting the further sophistication of administration, policing and security, the additional helping of culture and control – and all this for our greater good! At least in the clandestine squandering of the cash, we are spared all these dubious blessings.

Ceronetti: 'One silly idea currently doing the rounds: what good things we could do with all the money that's spent! In fact, stupid and criminal as we are, we would certainly do worse things. The most expensive weapons are ones that are unusable as such: their utility lies precisely in the quantity of wealth sunk into them, which would otherwise unleash itself in other fields for the ruination of the earth and the degradation of its peoples. If, instead of millions of private cars, we built battle tanks, they would all end up in underground depots and our cities would be able to breathe.'

So, we shouldn't keep going on about corruption and embezzlement of all kinds (in any case, the recrimination is part of the crime). We should lucidly take the view that, from a rational point of view and a reasonable human perspective, there are no longer sufficient needs or useful ends to cope with such a mass of money and resources. Were it not for efficient, organized embezzlement, there is a danger we would be confronted with an excess of means and a shortage of ends – a grave and demoralizing situation which we must stave off with bankruptcies, waste, misuse of public funds, etc.

The only offender in all this, if we accept that the main function of money is to circulate and be spent, is the small saver. For whereas the big financial crooks merely contravene the moral law or legality, he contravenes the immoral law, the profound law of our society . . . Saving, the retention of monies, the unlawful imprisonment of private funds which could be put to public use, that is to say which could become liquid capital – that is where real corruption lies today. And it is only right that the law should come down on the small saver at the same time as it grants an amnesty to the large-scale fraudsters and gives the green light to their operations.

19 February 1996

Disneyworld Company

In the early 1980s, when the iron and steel industry of Lorraine went into irreversible decline, the authorities had the idea of cushioning the collapse by creating a European leisure park, an 'intelligent' theme park intended to re-inject some dynamism into the region. It was called Smurfland.[31] The managing director of the defunct steelworks became, quite naturally, the managing director of the theme park and the unemployed steelworkers were re-employed as 'Smurfmen'. Sadly, when the park itself had for various reasons to close its doors, the ex-steelworkers found themselves unemployed once again. A grim destiny which made them, first, real victims of the world of work, then phantom victims of leisure, then, in the end, cast-offs from both spheres.

But Smurfland was merely a miniature. The Disney enterprise is on quite another scale. To get some idea of it, you have to know that Disney 'Unlimited', after taking over one of the biggest American TV channels, is currently buying up

31. Strictly speaking, it was called Schtroumpfland, but was largely known as Smurfland in the UK (*les Schtroumps* = the Smurfs).

42nd Street in New York, the 'red light district' of 42nd Street, to turn it into a kind of erotic amusement zone, without changing it in any – significant – way. It is merely transforming a mecca of pornography, *in situ*, into a subsidiary of Disneyworld. Transforming the pornographers and the prostitutes, like the Smurfland steelworkers, into extras in their own world, all metamorphosed into something identical, into museum pieces, Disney characters. And do you know how General Schwarzkopf, architect of the US Gulf War strategy, celebrated his 'victory'? With a gigantic party at Disneyworld. Such revellings in the mecca of the imagination were surely a worthy conclusion to that virtual war.

But the Disney enterprise goes further than the imagination. The great precursor, the initiator of the virtual reality of the imagination, is currently taking over the whole of the real world to incorporate it into its synthetic world in the form of an immense 'reality show', in which it is reality itself which presents itself as spectacle, in which the real itself becomes a theme park. A reality transfusion, the way we speak of blood transfusions. Except, in this case, it is a transfusion of real blood into the bloodless universe of the virtual.

They are even rebuilding an exact replica of Disneyland Los Angeles at Disneyworld in Orlando. Like a kind of second-level attraction, a simulacrum raised to the second power. This is the same job as CNN did on the Gulf War – the prototype of the event which did not take place because it took place in real time, in the instantaneity of CNN. Today, Disney might well restage the Gulf War as a global attraction. Christmas at Eurodisney was celebrated with the Red Army choirs. Everything is possible, everything can be recycled in the polymorphous world of the virtual. Nothing is irredeemable. There is no real reason why Disney should not buy up the human genome, which is currently being sequenced, to turn it into a genetic attraction. Why not cryogenize the whole planet, exactly as Walt Disney had himself cryogenized in liquid nitrogen, with a view to some kind of resurrection or other in the real world? But there no longer is a real world, and there won't be one – not even for Walt Disney: if he wakes up one day he'll get the shock of his life. In the meantime, from the depths of his liquid nitrogen he goes on annexing the world – both imaginary and real – subsuming it into the spectral universe of virtual reality in which we have all become extras. The difference is that, as we slip on our data suits or our sensors, or tap away at our keyboards, we are moving into living spectrality, whereas he, the brilliant precursor, has moved into the virtual reality of death.

The New World Order is a Disneyish order. But Disney is not alone in this kind of attractive cannibalism. We've seen Benetton draw on all the immediacy of the human drama in its advertising campaigns (AIDS, Bosnia, poverty, apartheid) by transfusing reality into the New Media Figuration at the point where misery and commiseration come to resonate together interactively. The virtual buys up the real 'as is' and serves it up just so: 'ready-to-go'.

If this operation can be successful on such a scale, without incurring anything but moral disapproval, and indeed arousing universal fascination, this is because reality itself, the world itself, with all its frenetic clone activity, has already transformed itself into an interactive performance, into a kind of Lunapark of ideologies, technologies, works, knowledge – and even of death and destruction. All just right for cloning and resuscitation in an infantile museum of the Imagination, in a virtual museum of Information.

Similarly, there's no point looking for computer viruses. We are all caught up in the viral interconnection of systems, and it is information itself which is the virus, not yet transmitted sexually, but much more effectively conducted along digital channels.

So Disney merely has to stoop down to pick up reality as it is. 'Built-in spectacle', as Guy Debord would say. But we are no longer in the society of the spectacle, which has itself become a spectacular concept. It is no longer the contagion of spectacle which alters reality, it is the contagion of the virtual which obliterates the spectacle. With its diverting, distancing effects, Disneyland still represented spectacle and folklore, but with Disneyworld and its tentacular extension, we are dealing with a generalized metastasis, with a cloning of the world and of our mental universe, not in the imaginary register, but in the viral and the virtual. We are becoming not alienated, passive spectators, but interactive extras, the meek, freeze-dried extras in this immense reality show. This is no longer the spectacular logic of alienation, but a spectral logic of disembodiment; not a fantastic logic of diversion, but a corpuscular logic of transfusion, transubstantiation of each of our cells. An undertaking of radical deterrence of the world, then, but from the inside this time, not from outside, as we saw in what is now the almost nostalgic world of capitalist reality. In virtual reality the extra is no longer either an actor or a spectator; he is off-stage, he is a transparent operator.

And Disney wins on yet another level. Not content with obliterating the real by turning it into a 3-D, but depthless, virtual image, it obliterates time by synchronizing all periods, all cultures in the same tracking shot, by setting them alongside each other in the same scenario. In this way, it inaugurates real time — time as a single point, one-dimensional time, a thing which is also without depth: neither present, past nor future, but the immediate synchrony of all places and all times in the same timeless virtuality. The lapsing or collapsing of time: this is the real fourth dimension. The dimension of the virtual, of real time, the dimension which, far from superadding itself to the three dimensions of real space, obliterates them all. So it has been suggested that in a century or a millennium, the old 'swords and sandals' epics will be seen as actual Roman films, dating from the Roman period, as true documentaries on Antiquity; that the Paul Getty Museum at Malibu, a pastiche of a villa from Pompeii, will be confused anachronistically with a villa from the third century B.C. (as will the works inside: Rembrandt and Fra Angelico will all be jumbled together in the same flattening of time); and that the commemoration of the French Revolution at Los Angeles in 1989 will be confused retrospectively with the real event. Disney achieves the *de facto* realization of this timeless utopia by producing all events, past or future, on simultaneous screens, remorselessly mixing all the sequences as they would – or will – appear to a civilization other than our own. But this is already *our* civilization. It is already increasingly difficult for us to imagine the real, to imagine History, the depth of time, three-dimensional space – just as difficult as it once was, starting out from the real world, to imagine the virtual one or the fourth dimension.

4 March 1996

The Global and the Universal

Globalization and universality do not go together. Indeed, they might be said to be mutually exclusive. Globalization is the globalization of technologies, the market, tourism and information. Universality is the universality of values, human rights, freedoms, culture and democracy. Globalization seems irreversible; the universal might be said, by contrast, to be disappearing. At least as constituted as a system of values at the level of Western modernity, which is something that has no equivalent in any other culture. Even a living, contemporary culture like the Japanese has no term for it. No word to refer to a system of values which regards itself as attuned to all cultures and their difference but which, paradoxically, does not conceive itself as relative, and aspires, in all ingenuousness, to be the ideal transcendence [*dépassement*] of all the others. We do not imagine for a moment that the universal might merely be the particular style of thinking of the West, its specific product – an original one, admittedly, but in the end no more exportable than any home-grown product. And yet, this is how the Japanese see it, as a specific, Western feature; and, far from signing up to an abstract concept, they, by a strange twist, relativize our universal and incorporate it into their singularity.

Every culture worthy of the name comes to grief in the universal. Every culture which universalizes itself loses its singularity and dies away. This is how it is with those we have destroyed by their enforced assimilation, but it is also how it is with ours in its pretension to universality. The difference is that the others died of their singularity, which is a fine death; whereas we are dying from the loss of all singularity, from the extermination of all our values, which is an ignoble death. We believe the fate of every value is to be elevated to universality, without gauging the mortal danger that promotion represents: far rather than an elevation, that process represents a reduction or, alternatively, an elevation to the degree zero of value. In Enlightenment times, universalization occurred at the top, by an upward progression. Today, it happens at the bottom, by a neutralization of values due to their proliferation and indefinite extension. This is how it is with human rights, democracy, etc. Their expansion corresponds to their weakest definition, their maximum entropy. Degree Xerox of value. In fact, the universal perishes in globalization. Once it is turned into a reality, the dynamic of the universal as transcendence, as ideal goal, as utopia, ceases to exist as such. The globalization of trade puts an end to the universality of values. It is the triumph of *la pensée unique* over universal thought.[32]

What first becomes globalized is the market, the promiscuity of all exchanges and products, the perpetual flow of money. In cultural terms, it is the promiscuity of all signs and values or, in other words, pornography. For the worldwide broadcasting

32. '*La pensée unique*' has in recent years become one of the watchwords of French political discussion. It implies a single-track thinking of the kind once referred to in Britain by the acronym TINA ('There is no alternative'). The editor of *Le Monde diplomatique* has defined it as 'the translation into ideological terms . . . of the interests of a set of economic forces, in particular those of international capital' (Ignacio Ramonet, 'La pensée unique', *Le Monde diplomatique*, no. 490, January 1995).

and parading of anything and everything over the networks is pornography. No need for sexual obscenity; this interactive copulation suffices. At the end of this process there is no longer any difference between the global and the universal. The universal itself is globalized: democracy and human rights circulate like any other global product – like oil or capital.

Given all this, we may ask ourselves whether the universal has not already succumbed to its own critical mass, and if it has ever had anything but lip-service paid to it, or been honoured anywhere but in official moralities. At any rate, for us the mirror of the universal is shattered (we can, in fact, see in this something like the mirror-stage of humanity). But perhaps this is fortunate, for, in the fragments of this broken mirror, all the singularities re-emerge. The ones we thought threatened survive, the ones we thought had disappeared revive. The case of Japan is, once again, quite remarkable in this connection. Japan has achieved its (technical, economic and financial) globalization better than any other country, but has done so *without passing through the universal* (the succession of bourgeois ideologies and forms of political economy) and without losing anything of its singularity, despite what is said. We may even suppose that it was as a result of not being encumbered by the universal that it has had such global, technical success, directly combining the singular (the power of ritual) with the global (virtual power).

The increasingly intense resistances to globalization – social and political resistances, which may seem like an archaic rejection of modernity at all costs – have to be seen as harbouring an original defiant reaction to the sway of the universal. Something which goes beyond the economic and the political. A kind of *painful revisionism* in respect of the established positions of modernity, in respect of the idea of progress and history – a kind of rejection not only of the famous global technostructure, but of the mental structure of the identification of all cultures and all continents in the concept of the universal. This resurgence – or even insurrection – of singularity may assume

violent, anomalous, irrational aspects from the viewpoint of 'enlightened' thought –
it may take ethnic, religious or linguistic forms, but also, at the individual level, may
find expression in character disorders or neuroses. But it would be a basic error (the
very error one sees emerging in the moral orchestration of the politically correct discourse common to all the powers-that-be and to many 'intellectuals') to condemn all
these upsurges out of hand as populist, archaic or even terroristic. Everything which
constitutes an event today is done against the universal, against that abstract universality (and this includes the frantic antagonism of Islam to Western values: it is because
it is the most vehement protest against this Western globalization that Islam today is
public enemy number one). If we will not understand this, then we will be caught up
in an endless and pointless wrangle between a universal thought assured of its power
and good conscience and an ever greater number of implacable singularities. Even in
our societies which are acculturated to the universal, one can see that none of what
has been sacrificed to this concept has really disappeared. It has simply gone underground. And what is now running backwards is a whole self-styled progressive
history, a whole evolutionism crystallized on its end-point – an end-point which has,
in fact, been lost sight of in the meantime. That utopia has fallen apart today and its
deep-level dislocation is advancing even more quickly than its consolidation by force.

We have before us a complex three-term arrangement: there is the globalization
of exchanges, the universality of values and the singularity of forms (languages, cultures, individuals and characters, but also chance, accident, etc. – all that the
universal, in keeping with its law, impugns as an exception or anomaly). Now, as
universal values lose some of their authority and legitimacy, the situation changes
and becomes more radical. So long as they could assert themselves as mediating
values, they were (more or less well) able to integrate the singularities as differences,
in a universal culture of difference. However, as triumphant globalization sweeps
away all differences and all values, ushering in a perfectly in-different (un)culture,

they can no longer do this. And once the universal has disappeared, all that remains is the all-powerful global technostructure standing over against the singularities which have reverted to the wild state and been thrown back on their own devices.

The universal has had its historical chance. But today, confronted with a new world order to which there is no alternative, with an irrevocable globalization on the one hand and the wayward drift or tooth-and-nail revolt of singularities on the other, the concepts of liberty, democracy and human rights cut a very pale figure indeed, being merely the phantoms of a vanished universal. And it is hard to imagine the universal rising from its ashes or to believe that things can be sorted out by the mere play of politics – this latter being caught up in the same deregulation and having barely any more substance to it than intellectual or moral power.

Matters are not, however, finally settled, even if it is now all up with universal values. In the void left by the universal, the stakes have risen, and globalization isn't certain to be the winner. In the face of its homogenizing, solvent power, we can see heterogeneous forces springing up all over, forces which are not only different, but antagonistic and irreducible.

18 March 1996

Deep Blue or the
Computer's Melancholia

The clash between a human being and an 'intelligent' artefact (Kasparov against Deep Blue) is highly symbolic, not only on account of the prestige of the game of chess, but because it sums up the dilemma of human beings where all our contemporary machines are concerned: computers, virtual or cybernetic devices, networks, etc. Behind the instrumental, creative or interactive use we make of such machines, there is, at bottom, always a clash, a challenge, a match, a duel, in which one of the parties may be checkmated or lose face. There is no interactivity with machines (any more, in fact, than there is with human beings: that is the illusion of communication). The interface does not exist. There is always, behind the apparent innocence of the technology, an issue of rivalry and control. The game of chess merely carries this situation to extremes.

So, in the end, Kasparov beat the computer, and everyone was greatly relieved, since in a way the honour of the species was at stake. Even if human intelligence will one day have to admit defeat, that moment must be postponed for as long as possible. And this is what makes this victory somewhat ambiguous, for even if it was not rigged (and it certainly wasn't), Kasparov could not – at all costs – not win. Man dreams with all his might of inventing a machine which is superior to himself, while at the same time he cannot conceive of not remaining master of his creations. He can no more do this than God could. Could God have envisaged creating man superior to himself and confronting him in a decisive combat (with Deep Blue, Kasparov was more or less pitting himself against a technical divinity, a technical superego divine in essence)? Yet that is what we do with our cybernetic creations, and we offer them a chance to beat us. Or, rather, it is our dream that they should surpass us – and do this, of course, as a mark of our power, though we cannot bear this either. So, man is trapped in the utopian aspiration of having a double superior to himself, but one he nonetheless has to beat to save face. God himself, defeated by his own creature, would have committed suicide. Moreover, on the only occasion on which human beings really stood up to him, in the Tower of Babel episode, he immediately cut their supply lines, in the form of language and mutual understanding. If computers were in danger of gaining the upper hand, should we not spread the same confusion among artificial languages as God did among natural ones? But we know that the diversity of language eventually became man's privilege and his absolute weapon. It is, in a way, thanks to that diversity that human beings got the better of God by inventing multiple worlds and divinities, each in the image of their respective languages.

But, to come back to Kasparov, if he won, it was surely because he is (metaphorically) capable of speaking more than one language: that of the emotions, of intuition, of the stratagem, in a word, the language of play – not to mention the language of calculation. Whereas Deep Blue speaks only the language of calculation. The day this latter language prevails, in whatever form, Kasparov will be beaten. The day man himself speaks only that single language – the language of computers – he will be beaten.

In terms of play, man is neither inferior nor superior to God: he has managed to keep up a kind of rivalry and open game. This is what we can best hope for.

Balthazar Grácian said that God's strategy is to keep man eternally in suspense. But the proposition is reversible and we too keep Him in suspense. It is the same in the confrontation between natural and artificial intelligence: the rivalry is ultimately irresolvable, and the best thing is for the match to be eternally postponed.

The possible victory of the computer poses no problem: we know it can be due only to calculating power. The interesting question is: what makes Kasparov win? The first answer is given by Kasparov himself when he says, 'I play without thinking. My hands move faster than my thinking.' Clearly, Deep Blue has no hands to move faster than its thinking. It can only think fast. Now, it is a feature of human beings that they move faster than their thinking, thanks to something relating to their bodies, their sex, and which, in a way, does not even pass through the black box of the brain. You can call it affect, intuition, strategy. You can call it 'psychology'. But it isn't so much a question of any 'psychical' faculties which man might possess in addition to his mental faculties of calculation. The basic difference is that, for Kasparov, there is an opponent, another party. For Deep Blue, there is nothing out there – no other, no opponent. It moves within the confines of its own programme. The same applies here, relatively speaking, as with 'Desert Storm': for the Gulf War computers, there were no others, no Iraqis, no enemies (not even any Americans, in the end); the whole thing was played out in a closed circuit on the basis of calculation.

Now, it is precisely at this point, beyond the mental power of calculation, that the human being can expect to be definitively superior – in that relationship of otherness which is based on relinquishment of his own thought. This relinquishment, which Deep Blue will never know, is the subtle assumption of game-playing. It is here that the human being can impose himself through illusion, decoy, challenge, seduction and sacrifice. It is this strategy of not going the full hog, of playing within one's capabilities, that the computer understands least well, since it is condemned to play at the height of its capabilities. This syncopation or ellipsis of presence by which you provoke the emergence of the other – even in the form of the virtual ego of the computer – is real game-player's thinking. Kasparov himself has spoken (to ask that it be taken account of in the time on the clocks) of this 'dead time of the real during which he really thinks'. That is to say, during which he is mentally absent, while the other party, Deep Blue, is sunk in calculation. The human being takes this distraction of thought, this 'dead time', from his available time, whereas the computer does not divert a single second from its own calculating time. But, paradoxically, it is this which turns round against it. Kasparov insists on the fact that after his first defeat (but doubtless you have always to know to lose the first game), he played against his own nature, 'within himself', to entrap his adversary (this is just like *The Diary of a Seducer*). He learns to play weak moves, to simplify or close up the game. Clearly, with a simulacrum, you have to play against nature, to simulate better than it does and catch it out, catch it out by simulation which, for it, is merely the simulation of calculation, whereas for human beings it is an ironic power.

When up against the machine they have themselves programmed (let us not forget that it was men like Kasparov who programmed Deep Blue), human beings can only subtly de-programme themselves, become 'technically incorrect' to stay ahead of the game. They may even have to take over the machine's own place. Like the illusionist who had invented an automaton which imitated human being so well that, on stage, he was himself forced to become mechanical and mimic the automaton to maintain the distinction. This is the only possible strategy: if you become technically correct, you are unfailingly beaten by the machine.

There is another factor favouring human supremacy here: this is the basic symbolic rule which states that no player can be bigger than the game itself. The player must not be unbeatable, or the game may die. The player is mortal; the rules alone are immortal. Now the absolute aim of the machine (its secret ambition perhaps?) is to be perfect, unbeatable and immortal. Which shows it has understood nothing of the very essence of game-playing, and for that reason it will always be beaten in the end, if not by the opponent, at least by the game itself.

So there is little sense in predicting the certain victory of the machine in 2005, on the grounds that man has only cumulative knowledge, whereas the machine has exponential knowledge. For if the computer's knowledge is exponential, its thinking is not – which condemns it to a kind of exponential stability: at each move, it goes back to zero and goes through all the operations again. Whereas man, who filters the data, and actively considers only a few of what is actually an immense number of possibilities, is capable of extrapolating the data in a single direction, without regard for the initial state. He thus has truly exponential thought at his command, thought which is creative of unprecedented, unpredictable constellations – a kind of chaotic strategy which even a computer a thousand times more powerful than Deep Blue could not match up to. Against the computer, man personifies, as it were, the infinity of complexity, which is not the infinity of calculation, and which is perhaps closer to the infinity of chance (it would in fact be interesting to confront the computer with a game of chance or, in other words, a probabilistic disorder, which is different from human disorder. Where would it find a winning formula?)

The machine may, then, be unbeatable at all kinds of operations, but, where the essence of play is concerned, it is forever disadvantaged – forever out of the game. To have access to that essence, the machine would have had to have invented it, would have had to have been able to invent the very arbitrariness of the rules, which is unimaginable. And it is too late for this. More generally, to be a match for man, the machine would have had to have invented him – and it is too late for that too. In a desperate effort to look like him, or compete with him, the only remaining possibility is accident: an accident of calculation – and making a strategy out of that. Or suicide.

Man has invented machines which work, move and think better than him, or think for him. He has never invented any which could take pleasure or suffer in his stead. Nor even which can play better than he can. Which perhaps explains why computers get such deep blues.

1 April 1996

The Racing Driver and his Double

Formula One is a rather good example of the era of performance, in which the heights achieved are the work of man and machine simultaneously, each propelling the other to extremes without it being really clear which is the engine of this meteoric advance and which merely the other's double.

If man is haunted by the evil genius of technology, which pushes him to the limits – and even beyond his capabilities – then technology is haunted by man, who identifies with it and projects all his passions into it. The alliance between the two, the pact between them, can be brought about only through an excessive expenditure, a spectacular sacrifice. In Formula One, the two are reconciled by speed – the phantasm, the spectre, the ecstasy of speed – which has become an unstoppable, undeniable collective passion.

Viewed in machine terms, Formula One looks like a pyramid: a pyramidal synthesis of the efforts of thousands of people which culminate in a single car, a single man, a single brief, dazzling moment. The condensation is extreme, and the mirror of the race refracts all the energies deployed – energies all working towards one goal – into the performance of a single man, or rather into a two-sided confrontation, the intensity and brevity of which have nothing to do with the accumulation of effort and the extent of the infrastructure. The collective fascination with the race certainly owes much to this transfiguration of all into one. But this pyramid, of which the driver is simply the tip, is projected in its turn through the media and television on to millions of people – a gigantic redirection, a spectacular superstructure (even leaving out of account the commercial and promotional aspects of the operation). High concentration, then high dilution. In this way, Formula One encapsulates a whole – collective, technical and imaginary – cycle.

The driver, for his part, is alone. In his cockpit he no longer is anyone. He merges with his double, with the car, and so no longer has an identity of his own. He is a bit like Italo Calvino's *Non-existent Knight* in his armour. And he does not see the others, the other tournament knights. 'You don't have to like them or respect them,' said Alain Prost, 'when the green light comes on, they don't exist. I know I'm going to do battle with a Williams, a Lotus or a Ferrari.' The only time they see each other, when they really *feel* like adversaries, is on the start line, in pole position or just behind – the most dramatic moment, when often the race is decided on a single reflex in a perilous moment of dicing with a rival in close combat. After that, car and driver are merely a living projectile, whose purpose is to reach the goal. Keep your sights fixed on the podium. A Grand Prix is very much an obstacle race these days, with one's opponents among the obstacles, together with the rain, the state of the tyres and unpredictable accidents. A perpetual calculation. The projectile has to be constantly regulated, corrected. Only in appearance is the circuit the site of the competition. The competition takes place elsewhere – on the world car market, in the drivers' popularity charts, in advertising and the star system. The race takes place on a screen, the screen of speed. For, in these extreme reaches, speed is no longer exactly a spatial dimension but a screen on which the driver has to move with the dexterity of a teleconductor. 'As the fans can imagine, the real pleasure of driving has, if we are honest about it, practically disappeared.' The erosion of one's own pleasure is the price to be paid for shifting up from movement to pure speed, from the body in movement to the screen of speed. There is no passion in this – except the passion for winning, of course, though that is not a personal, but an operational passion. It shows up in the driver's brain the way the technical data show on the dashboard. It is in-built in the technical object itself, which is made to win, and which incorporates the driver's will as one of the technical elements required for victory. This seems inhuman, but to be honest about it, it is the mental logic of the race.

Having said this, at 180 mph, there is calm. This is the equivalent of the eye of the storm, the stasis of speed, the trance-like state: you are no longer in the same world (more modestly, you can achieve this same sensation in a normal car at over 125 mph). The background becomes definitively televisual, the physical perception of the other cars fades; you are in the pure event of speed; the perception of space becomes a tactile, reflex perception (in McLuhan's sense: the car becomes a tactile, tactical extension of the human body). There is no longer any reference here to a real landscape, or to competition or prestige: you pass into virtual imagery. You approach real time, the instantaneity of motion – but also, of course, catastrophe.

And here might be said to lie the other passion – alongside the passion for winning – a passion both more spectacular and murkier. Connected, admittedly, with the dramatization of the danger by the media, but also, more profoundly, with the symbolic rule of the challenge and the duel: the passion for accidents and death. There was a time when not just the drivers, but the spectators too, risked their lives on the circuits. Those sacrificial days are gone. As the personal pleasure in driving is gradually disappearing from the circuits, so too is the personal risk of death. Death is no longer anything but a virtual imaginary element. Only the cars die, only the engines are driven to destruction. Only the technical 'double' dies, which reinforces the abstract nature of the race. Admittedly, everyone dreams of it (which is not to say that they desire it), but the spectacle of death, shown 'live', is unacceptable today. However, the definitive elimination of accidents is unthinkable, as unthinkable as the absence of spectators. Even if the real spectators are only a tiny part of the virtual (television) audience, they are there. Even if the real risk is tiny in relation to the imaginary risk, it is there. And this dimension is absolutely vital. Without any random factor, without incident, expurgated of all its unpredictable elements, motor racing would lose all interest.

So the Formula One driver has a dual status: he is both an automatic terminal of the most refined technical machinery, a technical operator, and he is the symbolic operator of crowd passions and the risk of death. The paradox is the same for the motor companies, caught as they are between investment and potlatch. Is all this a calculated – and hence rational – investment (marketing and advertising)? Have we here a mighty commercial operation, or is the company spending inordinate sums, far beyond what is commercially viable, to assuage a passion for prestige and charisma (there is also a manufacturers' world championship)? In this confrontation between manufacturers, isn't there an excessive upping of the stakes, a dizzying passion, a delirium? This is certainly the aspect which appeals, in the first instance, to the millions of viewers. In the end, the average TV viewer has doubtless never been aware that McLaren is a flagship for Honda. And I am not sure he or she is tempted to play the Formula One driver in ordinary life. The impact of Formula One lies, then, in the exceptional and mythic character of the event of the race and the figure of the driver, and not in the technical or commercial spin-offs. It is not clear why speed would be both severely limited and morally condemned in the public domain and, at the same time, celebrated in Formula One as never before, unless there is an effect of sublime compensation going on here. Formula One certainly serves to popularize the cult of the car and its use, but it does much more to maintain the passion for absolute difference – a fundamental illusion for all, and one which jus-tifies all the excesses.

In the end, however, hasn't it gone about as far as it can? Isn't it close to a final state, a final perfection, in which all the cars and drivers, given the colossal resources deployed, would, in a repetitive scenario, achieve the same maximum performance and produce the same pattern in each race? If Formula One were merely a rational, industrial performance, a test-bed for technical possibilities, we should have to pre-dict that it would simply burn itself out. On the other hand, if Formula One is a spectacle, a collective, passionate (though perfectly artificial) event, embracing the multiple screens of technological research, the living prosthesis of the driver, and the television screens into which the viewers project themselves, then it certainly has a very fine future.

In a word, Formula One is a monster. Such a concentration of technology, money, ambition and prestige is a monster (as is the world of *haute couture*, which is equally abstract, and as far removed from real clothing as Formula One is from road traffic). Now, monsters are doomed to disappear, and we are afraid they might be disappearing. But we are not keen, either, to see them survive in a domesticated, routinized form. In an era of daily insignificance – including the insignificance of the car and all its constraints – we want at least to save the passion of a pure event, and exceptional beings who are permitted to do absolutely anything.

March 1995

Ruminations for
Spongiform Encephala

The mad cow epidemic is, first and foremost, a softening of human brains on an epidemic scale, with populations of human beings reeling in panic in a massive out–break of bovine mimicry. What we have before us is a full-scale test of the quality of the human herd.

There is no danger of cattle passing on their spongiform disease to us. It is already all around us, a mental virus far more harmful than the biological one. If our news and information system is itself the area most seriously affected (whatever *it* says about that), there is good reason: it is because that system represents an ideally sensitive target-area for the whole epidemic. The communications networks are a huge viral system and instant transmission is, in itself, a lethal danger. In this per–petual critical-mass situation, the slightest spark is sufficient to prick the abscess of collective responsibility, just as the tiniest body projected into a diffuse solution brings about lightning-quick crystallization.

Our systems secrete such a charge of floating responsibility that this condenses from time to time as static electricity does in lightning. To the real threats we face, we must also add this vast store of responsibility, this radioactive cloud awaiting the

slightest chance to burst. The mad cow is a reincarnation of the sacred cow as rot-
ting cow. Unlike the Indian example, where the sacred animal shares infectious
diseases with human beings but does so in endemic mode, cattle doomed to the
butcher's knife take their revenge by shifting from the endemic to the epidemic.
Cows have never come to terms with being fed rotten sheep carcases and so turned
into carnivores. In spite of their own tranquil obliviousness, they have never come
to terms with being turned into butcher's meat for a single species, which remained
entirely oblivious of the break thus created with the rest of the animal kingdom.
Cows have never come to terms with being turned into simulacra, as, in keeping
with this carnivorous ideal, has recently been the case. For everything about them
is programmed now: by hormones, transplants, the genetic redistribution of parts
of the body, by way of a plastic surgery aimed at maximum profitability of the
animal as meat. The cow is not what it once was. It is an artefact, a kind of dis-
embodied meat, which takes its suicidal revenge by infecting its predator. This is the
vengeance cows have been ruminating.

It is because the body of the cow has become a non-body, a meat-machine, that
the viruses lay hold of it. It is because our human bodies have become non-bodies –
neuronal, operational machines – that they have lost their immunity and the viruses
are laying hold of them. And it is also because computing has become purely a matter
of media technology that it has become vulnerable to all the viruses of information.
All viruses are in league: from the prion which infects the cow to the cow which
infects man, and to man who infects the whole planet (to the point of infiltrating
himself into his own genetic code to modify it). Perhaps there is a secret purpose in
all this? Who can know what subterranean processes of revolt and vengeance exist
among those beings we have doomed to imprisonment and butchery?

The biological virus in a sense 'knows' that it can avail itself of the technical virus
of computing and the mental virus of brain-softening to spread itself and gain total

revenge. Studies had already shown cattle – and, indeed, all ruminants – to be the main destroyers of the ozone layer, with their sulphurous farting, their poisonous flatulence. So, the conspiracy has been going on for quite some time! There is no point imputing all this to anyone in particular: collective madness is a pyramidal synthesis of convergent effects, of phenomena in resonance.

From the protein to the cow's brain, from that brain to our information systems, from those systems and networks to the automatic mental decoder of opinion and on into the spongiform encephalon of the political class, the structure is the same, and therefore allows exponential development to occur. Let us run back along this chain from the other end: there is nothing now to protect politicians from the virus of opinion; but nothing protects that opinion from the virus of information; nothing protects our computerized information system from the tiniest little news story or from its own hysteria; and, for mysterious reasons, what protected the cow from the prion seems to have disappeared too. There is total immunodeficiency from one end of the chain to the other. And so it is that in an allegedly rational system, chaos can grow exponentially, producing massive effects of collective intoxication wholly out of proportion with the initial conditions.

AIDS, terrorism, the stock market crash, computer viruses, natural catastrophes: all these phenomena are correlated and conform to the same protocol of virulence. They are wholly consistent with each other, and with the banality of the system. For example, a single terrorist act forces us to review the whole political scene in the light of terrorism. The mere appearance of AIDS, even at a statistically low level, forces us to review the whole spectrum of disease and the body in the light of the viral, immunodeficiency hypothesis, etc. So, the appearance of mad cows is the equivalent of a terrorist act.

There is savage irony in the fact of cows providing the litmus test, so to speak, for the European political situation (when even the massacre in Bosnia had not managed to disturb its incoherent, hypocritical state). So, British public opinion can only either turn on its government, as guilty of negligence, or on a Europe allegedly seeking to impose its law on the country. An immediate boost for all nationalisms: 'Spongiform or not, they're *our* cows!' When a situation is rotten and contradictory, the tiniest incident reveals all its rottenness and contradictoriness. Even the rottenness and contradictoriness of the liberal system. 'Everything must circulate freely' – well, so then must germs, viruses, drugs, capital and terrorists. And this circulation of the worst of things is much quicker than the circulation of the best. There will be no end, then, to the opening and re-closing of frontiers.

History itself argues in favour of the terrorist hypothesis where mad cow disease is concerned, the Turin European summit on spongiform encephalopathy following on from that at Sharm-el-Sheik on Islamic terrorism. Except that the wobbly solidarity of the Europeans around the eradication of this threat was even more pitiful and Ubuesque than the world parade of heads of State assembled to do battle with a phantom enemy. The British mad cow and the Palestinian kamikaze bomber are all part of the same struggle, then: they share the same suicidal energy, the same unfathomable hatred. And even the prion is in on it. From what genetic abyss has that protein arisen? Where does the international terrorist plot originate? And what is the meaning of this sequence: the prion infecting the cow, the cow infecting the media, the media driving the masses to hysteria – all victims of each other and, at the same time, all colluding towards maximum catastrophic effect.

Seen from the angle of the serial deregulation of the system, the success is total. Who is harmed by any of this? The masses finally have a distraction from their dull lives and the powers-that-be have a way to distract attention from their wicked ones. However, through such events, the social order loses credibility by the day. Not being 'personally' responsible for anything (as in the contaminated blood affair), the governing classes are all the more impotent in the face of the indiscernible consequences of the event. Admittedly, they can fight the symptoms – slaughter cows or eradicate terrorists – but they will have great problems breaking the chain of events which has led up to this point, the epidemic of circumstances and objective conditions which have themselves colluded in the catastrophe. The powers-that-be understand nothing of the 'perverse' processes of virality, in which even calming and prophylactic measures – the excess of prophylactic measures – merely increase the panic. And there is another 'perverse' variable – the media. Accused as scapecows, they protest that they are only doing their job. But it is precisely in doing their job (which was, we might remember, the excuse of the concentration camp officials) that they are most solidly in the viral loop.

Doubtless, the next world summit will be against earthquakes – with the same success. And there is no doubt, either, that this storm whipped up by the collusion between a cow and a protein will end in a beating of butterfly wings – that is to say, in no perceptible change to the order of things. But, in the meanwhile, it will have revealed the secret disorder, the colossal disorder of our systems, the threat of imminent failure by which they are constantly beset. This at least can be chalked up to the event, not to mention the useful finding that human livestock teeters on the brink of the same fate as mad cows, and that the brain-softening effect of news and information is every bit the equal of spongiform encephalopathy. And not counting, also, the secret delight there is in panic, even for those who are panicking, the (aesthetic) pleasure in the absurd disproportion of the event, and the pleasure generated by the impotence of a system grappling with its own viruses.

15 April 1996

Screened Out

Video, interactive screens, multimedia, the Internet, virtual reality – we are threatened on all sides by interactivity. What was separated in the past is now everywhere merged; distance is abolished in all things: between the sexes, between opposite poles, between stage and auditorium, between the protagonists of action, between subject and object, between the real and its double. And this confusion of terms, this collision of poles means that nowhere – in art, morality or politics – is there now any possibility of a moral judgement. With the abolition of distance – of the 'pathos of distance' – everything becomes undecidable. And this is true even in the physical realm: when the receiver and the source of a transmission are too close together, a feedback effect ensues which scrambles the transmission waves; when an event and the broadcasting of that event in real time are too close together, this renders the event undecidable and virtual, stripping it of its historical dimension and removing it from memory. Whether it is virtual technologies which create undecidability or our undecidable world which gives rise to these technologies is itself undecidable.

Wherever a mingling of this kind – a collision of poles – occurs, then the vital tension is discharged.

Even in 'reality' TV, where, in the live telling of the story, the immediate tele-visual acting, we see the confusion of existence and its double. There is no separation any longer, no empty space, no absence: you enter the screen and the visual image unhindered. You enter your life as you would walk on to a screen. You slip on your own life like a data suit.

Unlike photography, cinema and painting, in which there is a scene and a gaze, the video image – and the computer screen – induce a kind of immersion, a sort of umbilical relation, of 'tactile' interaction, as McLuhan, in his day, said of televi-sion. A cellular, corpuscular immersion: you enter the fluid substance of the image – possibly to modify it – in the same way as science infiltrates itself into the genome, the genetic code, to transform the body itself by that means. You move as you like, you make of the interactive image what you will, but immersion is the price to pay for this infinite availability, this open combinatorial of elements. It is the same with the 'virtual' text – any virtual text (the Internet, word-processing). This is worked on like a computer-generated image – something which no longer bears any relation to the transcendence of the gaze or of writing. At any rate, as soon as you are in front of the screen, you no longer see the text as text, but as image. Now, it is in the strict separation of text and screen, of text and image, that writing is an activity in its own right – never an interaction.

Similarly, it is only with the strict separation of stage and auditorium that the spectator is a participant in his/her own right. Everything today conspires to abol-ish that separation: the spectator being brought into a user-friendly, interactive immersion. The apogee of the spectator or his/her end? When all are actors, there is no action any longer, no scene. The end of the aesthetic illusion.

Machines produce only machines. This is increasingly true as the virtual tech-nologies develop. At a certain level of machination, of immersion in virtual machinery, there is no longer any man–machine distinction: the machine is on both sides of the interface. Perhaps you are indeed merely the machine's space now – the human being having become the virtual reality of the machine, its mirror operator. This has to do with the very essence of the screen. There is no 'through' the screen the way there is a 'through' the looking-glass or mirror. The dimensions of time itself merge there in 'real time'. And, the characteristic of any virtual surface being first of all to be there, to be empty and thus capable of being filled with anything, it is left to you to enter in real time into interactivity with the void.

Similarly, everything which is produced by way of machines is a machine. The texts, images, films, speech and programmes which come out of computers are machine products, and they bear the features of such products: they are artificially padded-out, face-lifted by the machine; the films are stuffed with special effects, the texts full of *longueurs* and repetitions due to the machine's malicious will to function at all costs (that is *its* passion), and the operator's fascination with this limitless possibility of functioning. Hence the wearisome character in films of all this violence and pornographied sexuality, which are merely special effects of violence and sex, no longer even fantasized by humans, but pure machinic violence which no longer even affects us. And this explains all these texts which resemble the work of 'intelligent' virtual agents, whose only act is the act of programming, the rest unfolding on purely automatic lines. This has nothing to do with *écriture automatique*, which played on the magical telescoping of words and concepts, whereas all we have here is the automatism of programming, an automatic run-through of all the possibilities. Roll on the machine design of the body, the text, the image. This is called cybernetics: controlling the image, the text, the body from within, as it were, from its matrix, by playing with its code or the genetic details. It is this phantasm of the ideal performance of the text or image, the possibility of correcting endlessly, which produce in the 'creative artist' this vertige of interactivity with his own object, alongside the anxious vertige at not having reached the technological limits of his possibilities. In fact, it is the (virtual) machine which is speaking you, the machine which is thinking you.

And is there really any possibility of discovering something in cyberspace? The Internet merely simulates a free mental space, a space of freedom and discovery. In fact, it merely offers a multiple, but conventional, space, in which the operator interacts with known elements, pre-existent sites, established codes. Nothing exists beyond these search parameters. Every question has its anticipated response. You are the automatic questioner and, at the same time, the automatic answering device of the machine. Both coder and decoder – in fact your own terminal, your own correspondent. That is the ecstasy of communication. There is no 'Other' out there and no final destination. And so the system goes on, without end and without purpose. And its sole potential is for infinite reproduction and involution. Hence the comfortable vertige of this electronic, computer interaction – like the vertige induced by drugs. You can spend your whole life at this, without a break. Drugs themselves are only ever the perfect example of a crazed, closed-circuit interactivity.

To win you over to it, they tell you the computer is merely a handier, more complex kind of typewriter. But this is not true. The typewriter is an entirely external object. The page flutters in the open air, and so do I. I have a physical relation to writing. I touch the blank or written page with my eyes – something I cannot do with the screen. The computer is a true prosthesis. I am not merely in an interactive relation with it, but a tactile, intersensory relation. I become, myself, an ectoplasm of the screen. And this, no doubt, explains, in this incubation of the virtual image and brain, the technical faults which afflict computers, and which are like the failings of one's own body.

On the other hand, the fact that identity is the identity of the network and never that of individuals, the fact that priority is given to the network rather than to the network's protagonists implies the possibility of hiding, of disappearing into the intangible space of the virtual, so that you are not detectable anywhere – even by yourself. This resolves all problems of identity, not to mention those of alterity. So, the attraction of all these virtual machines no doubt derives not so much from the thirst for information and knowledge as from the desire to disappear, and the possibility of dissolving oneself into a phantom conviviality. A kind of 'high', which takes the place of happiness, of obvious happiness, by the very fact that happiness no longer has any *raison d'être* here.

Virtuality comes close to happiness only because it surreptitiously removes all reference to things. It gives you everything, but at the same time it subtly deprives you of everything. The subject is realized to perfection, but when realized to perfection, the subject automatically becomes object, and panic sets in.

6 May 1996

The Art Conspiracy

Just as, amid all the pornography which surrounds us, we have lost the illusion of desire, so in contemporary art we have also lost the desire for illusion. In porn, there is no longer any room for desire. After the orgy and the liberation of all desires, we have moved into the transsexual, in the sense of a transparency of sex, into signs and images which obliterate the whole secret, the ambiguity of sex. Transsexual in the sense that sex now has nothing to do with the illusion of desire, but relates solely to the hyperreality of the image.

So it is with art, which has also lost the desire for illusion – preferring the elevation of everything to aesthetic banality – and has consequently become trans-aesthetic. For art, the orgy of modernity consisted in the exhilaration of deconstructing the object and representation. During that period, the aesthetic illusion was still very powerful, as is, for sex, the illusion of desire. The energy of sexual difference, which passes into all the figures of desire, has as its counterpart in art the energy of dissociation from reality (Cubism, abstraction, Expressionism), though each of these corresponds to a desire to pierce the secret of desire and the secret of the object. To the point where these two strong configurations, the scene of desire and the scene of illusion, disappear, giving way to the same transsexual, transaesthetic obscenity – the obscenity of visibility and of the inexorable transparency of everything. In reality, there is no longer any pornography identifiable as such, because the essence of the pornographic has passed into all the technologies of the visual and televisual spheres.

But perhaps, deep down, we are merely playing out the comedy of art, as other societies have played out the comedy of ideology, as Italian society, for example (though it is not the only one), plays out the comedy of power, as we play out the comedy of porn in the obscene advertising of the images of the female body. This perpetual striptease, these phantasies *à sexe ouvert*, this sexual blackmail – if it were all true, it would be genuinely unbearable. But fortunately it is all too obvious to be true. Transparency is too good to be true. As for art, it is too superficial to be really useless. There must be an underlying mystery. As with anamorphosis, there must be an angle from which all this useless orgy of sex and signs makes complete sense but, for the moment, we can only adopt an attitude of ironic indifference towards it. In this unreality of porn, this insignificance of art, there is something of the order of an underlying enigma, an inherent mystery. An ironic form of our destiny perhaps? If everything becomes too obvious to be true, perhaps there is still a chance for illusion. What lurks behind this falsely transparent world? Another sort of intelligence or a definitive lobotomy?

(Modern) art was able to be part of the *part maudite*, the 'accursed share', by being a sort of dramatic alternative to reality, by expressing the irruption of unreality into reality. But what can art mean now in a world that is hyperrealist from the outset, a world that is cool, transparent, image-conscious? What can porn mean in a world that is pornographied from the outset? What can they do but tip us a last paradoxical wink – that of reality mocking itself in its most hyperrealistic form, that of sex mocking itself in its most exhibitionistic form, that of art mocking itself and its own disappearance in its most artificial form: irony. The dictatorship of images is, in any event, an ironic dictatorship. But that irony itself is no longer part of the accursed share; it is, rather, party to insider-trading, to that hidden, shameful complicity which binds the artist, playing on his/her aura of derision, to the stupefied, incredulous masses. Irony, too, is a part of the art conspiracy.

Art playing on its own disappearance and the disappearance of its object was still an art of great works. But art playing at re-cycling itself indefinitely by helping itself to reality? Most contemporary art is engaged in just this: appropriating banality, the throwaway, mediocrity as value and as ideology. In these innumerable installations and performances, what is going on is merely a compromise with the state of things – and simultaneously with all the past forms of the history of art. An admission of unoriginality, banality and worthlessness, elevated into a perverse aesthetic value, if not indeed a perverse aesthetic pleasure. Admittedly, it is claimed that all this mediocrity is sublimated in the transition to the level of art, which is distanced and ironic. But it is just as worthless and insignificant at that level as before. Transition to the aesthetic level rescues nothing. In fact the opposite is true: it is mediocrity raised to the second power. It claims to be worthless: '*I'm worthless, I'm worthless!*' and it really is worthless!

We have here the whole duplicity of contemporary art: laying claim to worthlessness [*la nullité*], insignificance and non-meaning; aiming for worthlessness, when it is already worthless; aiming for non-meaning, when it already signifies nothing; claiming to achieve superficiality in superficial terms. Now, nullity is a secret quality which not everyone can aspire to. Insignificance – true insignificance, the victorious defiance of meaning, the stripping away of meaning, the art of the disappearance of meaning – is an exceptional quality possessed by a few rare works – works which never claim that quality.

There is an initiatory form of nullity, just as there is an initiatory form of the nothing, or an initiatory form of evil. And then there is insider-trading, the fakers of nullity, the snobbery of nullity, of all those who prostitute the Nothing for value, who prostitute Evil for useful ends. We must not let these fakers get away with it. When the Nothing shows up in signs, when Nothingness emerges at the very heart of the system of signs, that is the fundamental event of art. It is the proper task of poetry to raise the Nothing to the power of the sign – not the banality or indifference of the real, but the radical illusion. In this way, Warhol truly is a 'zero', in the sense that he reintroduces nothingness into the heart of the image. He turns nullity and insignificance into an event which he transforms into a fatal strategy of the image.

The others merely have a commercial strategy of nullity, to which they give a promotional form, the sentimental form of the commodity, as Baudelaire put it. They hide behind their own nullity and the metastases of the discourse on art, which works generously to promote this nullity as a value (among other things, a value on the art market, of course). In a sense, this is worse than nothing, because it means nothing and yet it exists all the same, giving itself every reason to exist. With this paranoia colluding with art, there is no room for critical judgement any more, but merely for an amicable, and inescapably convivial, participation in nullity. This is the art conspiracy and its primal scene, carried forward by all the private shows, hangings, exhibitions, restorations, collections, donations and speculations. It is a conspiracy which cannot be 'unhatched' in any known universe, since, behind the mystification of images, it has put itself beyond the reach of thought.

The other side of this trickery is the way people are bluffed into according importance and credence to all this, on the grounds that it is not possible that it should be so worthless and empty and there must be something to it. Contemporary art plays on this uncertainty, on the impossibility of a reasoned aesthetic value-judgement, relying on the guilt of those who simply cannot understand, or have not understood that there is nothing to understand. Here again, this is insider-trading.

But we may also take the view that these people, whom art keeps at bay, have indeed fully understood, since, by their very stupefaction, they show an intuitive understanding that they are victims of an abuse of power; that they are not being let in on the rules of the game; that the wool is being pulled over their eyes. In other words, art has made its entry into the general process of insider-trading (and not merely from the financial point of view of the art market, but in the very management of aesthetic values). In this it is not alone: the same kind of collusion is to be found in politics, the economy and information, with the same ironic resignation on the part of the 'consumers'.

'Our admiration for painting is the consequence of a long process of adaptation which has gone on over centuries, and exists for reasons which very often have nothing to do either with art or the mind. Painting created its receptor. It is, at bottom, a relationship of convention' (Gombrowicz to Dubuffet). The only question is how such a machine can continue to function in a situation of critical disillusionment and commercial frenzy. And if it can, how long will this illusionism, this occultism last? A hundred years? Two hundred? Will art have a second, interminable existence, like the secret services, which, though we know they have long had no secrets to steal or exchange, still thrive amid a superstitious belief in their usefulness, and continue to generate a mythology?

20 May 1996

TV Fantasies

Television has been in the news a lot lately. It is supposed to exist to speak to us about the world. And, like any self-respecting medium, it is also supposed to put events first and its own concerns second. But for some time now, it seems either to have lost this respect for itself or to have come to regard *itself* as the event.

Even the 'Guignols' on Canal Plus have started to target the confused goings-on in the little world of TV and radio, including those on their own channel.[33] Not to mention all the movements of star presenters, channel heads and programme directors between the different companies, and the intrigue and corruption which one supposes is endemic in that jungle, but which has now been transferred to the screen and is served up to the audience as a TV show in its own right.

There seemed little chance the media would escape the compulsive syndrome of investigation, whitewashing, rehabilitation and repentance the political class and big business have been going through for some time now. All forms of power are

33. Canal Plus's satirical puppet show 'Les Guignols de l'Info' has been running since 29 August 1988.

currently afflicted with the depressive syndrome of power – the justification complex which besets all power once it grows to excess and no longer has any representative function. This is the case with political power, and today also with media power. If television has begun to revolve around its own concerns and to engage endlessly in examining its own convulsions, this is because it is no longer capable of finding a meaning outside itself, of getting beyond itself as a medium, and finding its purpose: to produce the world as information and give meaning to that information. Through using and abusing events with images – to the point of coming under suspicion of conjuring events up out of nothing – television has become virtually disconnected from the world and has begun to turn back in on its own universe like a meaningless signifier, desperately seeking an ethic to replace its failing credibility, a moral status to replace its lack of imagination (once again, the same applies with the political class).

It is at this point that it begins to become corrupt. It is challenged on all sides and incapable of responding to the basic question, which is at the same time the major charge levelled against it: how do things stand with images and their meaning, how do things stand with the very myth of information and television which is everywhere trumpeted shamelessly? Where is your responsibility in all this? The media world as a whole, incapable of replying to these questions, or doubtless even of asking them, prefers to pick at its own sores, to put its own conflicts, rivalries, profligacy and bad management on show. But this is merely a diversion. Excessive pay deals, settlings of old scores, the polemic between public service broadcasting and the private companies – all these things which make the headlines today are merely masking the fundamental fact that television has lost both any idea of what it is doing and the ability to imagine the real world. As a result, it is talking only to itself or to an unidentified audience whose role is merely to provide viewing figures – which amounts to the same thing. It is consequently losing its credibility with the public, and losing all credit in its own eyes. In the light of the latest goings-on, it seems it no longer has any illusions about its own practices.

The vice here is circularity. The vice of the medium for the medium's sake, as in the past we had art for art's sake. It is the vice of all institutions which begin to operate autarkically, no longer showing any concern for their object or their function. Immense bachelor machines whose whole energy goes into fuelling and reproducing themselves. This is our dilemma, one that comes to us from the depths of simulation: what if the sign did not relate either to the object or to meaning, but to the promotion of the sign as sign? And what if information did not relate either to the event or the facts, but to the promotion of information itself as event? And more precisely today: what if television no longer related to anything except itself as message? This is where McLuhan's formulation can be seen to be absolutely brilliant: the medium has swallowed the message and it is this, the multi-medium, which is proliferating in all directions. And we are, indeed, seeing terrestrial and cable channels and services proliferating while actual programme content is disappearing and melting away – the TV viewer's almost involuntary channel-hopping here echoing television's own obsession with its own channels.

But this is not where the true corruption lies. The secret vice, already pointed out by Umberto Eco, lies in the way the media become self-referring and speak only among themselves. The *multimedium* is becoming the *intermedium*. This already problematic situation is aggravated when it is a single hypermedium – television – eyeing itself. All the more so as this tele-centrism is combined with a very severe implicit moral and political judgement: it implies that the masses basically neither need nor desire meaning or information – that all they ask for is signs and images. Television provides them with these in great quantities, returning to the real world, with utter – though well-camouflaged – contempt, in the form of 'reality shows' or vox-pops – that is to say, in the form of universal self-commentary and mocked-up scenarios, where both the questions and the answers are 'fixed'.

Of course, television is not alone in being confronted with this destiny – this vicious circle: the destiny of all those things which, no longer having an objective purpose, take themselves for their own ends. In so doing, they escape all responsibility, but also become bogged down in their own insoluble contradictions. This is, however, more particularly the critical situation of all the current media. Opinion polls themselves are a good example. They have had their moment of truth (as, indeed, did television), when they were the representative mirror of an opinion, in the days when such a thing still existed, before it became merely a conditioned reflex. But perpetual harassment by opinion polls has resulted in their being no longer a mirror at all; they have, rather, become a screen. A perverse exchange has been established between polls which no longer really ask questions and masses who no longer reply. Or rather they become cunning partners, like rats in laboratories or the viruses pursued in experiments. They toy with the polls at least as much as the polls toy with them. They play a double game. It is not, then, that the polls are bogus or deceitful, but rather that their very success and automatic operation have made them random. There is the same double game, the same perverse social relationship between an all-powerful, but wholly self-absorbed, television and the mass of TV viewers, who are vaguely scandalized by this misappropriation, not just of public money, but of the whole value system of news and information. You don't need to be politically aware to realize that, after the famous dustbins of history, we are now seeing the dustbins of information. Now, information may well be a myth, but this alternative myth, the modern substitute for all other values, has been rammed down our throats incessantly. And there is a glaring contrast between this universal myth and the actual state of affairs. The real catastrophe of television has been how deeply it has failed to live up to its promise of providing information –

its supposed modern function. We dreamed first of giving power – political power – to the imagination, but we dream less and less of this, if indeed at all. The fantasy then shifted on to the media and information. At times we dreamed (at least collectively, even if individually we continued to have no illusions) of finding some freedom there – an openness, a new public space. Such dreams were soon dashed: the media turned out to be much more conformist and servile than expected, at times more servile than the professional politicians. The latest displacement of the imagination has been on to the judiciary. Again this has been an illusion, since, apart from the pleasing whiff of scandal produced, this is also dependent on the media operation. We are going to end up looking for imagination in places further and further removed from power – from any form of power whatever (and definitely far removed from cultural power, which has become the most conventional and professional form there is). Among the excluded, the immigrants, the homeless. But that will really take a lot of imagination because they, who no longer even have an image, are themselves the by-products of a whole society's loss of imagination, of the loss of any social imagination. And this is indeed the point. We shall soon see it is no use trying to locate the imagination somewhere. Quite simply, because there no longer is any. The day this becomes patently obvious, the vague collective disappointment hanging over us today will become a massive sickening feeling.

3 June 1996

Of Course Chirac is Useless

As we know, compulsory revelling makes the year-end a severe ordeal. Even among those having a whale of a time, the spectre of abandonment looms. It is precisely here, in this staged euphoria, that the crucial question of the social bond arises. Is the human being a social being? Nothing could be less certain. And it seems much less certain when you hear the midnight howling, in every tongue, of the crowd on the Champs-Elysées. But is the human being in fact *a human being*? That is what everyone seems to be trying to prove to themselves with all these pathetic year-end initiatives (whatever will the end of the century be like?), forcing their excessive therapeutic attentions on the poor. The attention is therapeutic for the rich, of course, whom it rescues from depression, but there is also an excess of charitable zeal directed at the poor, which at times amounts to harassment, as, for example, when the homeless are driven into hostels against their wills, some of them preferring to live and die non-socially. Through this hypochondriacal emotion for these sick members and organs of a society which indulges all the while in the fantasy that it is the world's fourth largest power, we are keen to prove to ourselves that we are human. It would be nice if this pathos of automatic mourning of the Christmas holiday period could be swept up by the current cold front and fall in stalactites of frozen tears on all the prophets of other people's misery.

We find the same icy preoccupation at Notre-Dame, where to the exclusion of the poor and the transparency of the cold is added the televisual transparency of the omnipresent screens. Like the new Year-2000 cribs, these screens are everywhere, in all the naves and aisles – the pulpit being occupied by the camera equipment. If the Word was made flesh, then solid flesh today has melted into the screen. Cardinal Lustiger[34] might simply be a hologram – he might not even be there – and the mass might be a kind of barely interactive CD-Rom; a reality as virtual as the Virgin's Immaculate Conception. Outside, with the queues at the doors of the cathedral, we have a prefiguration of Paradise. But this is not at all interactive: rather it is directive and the police are in control. The crowd is funnelled in through barriers and searched by the security forces. Paradise is over-full, the church is saturated – there's a waiting list (there's some danger it may be like this at the gates of the real Paradise). For those who will not get in, the sound is relayed live in the icy wind. 'Unto you a Saviour is born'. But the original is inaccessible. It's like the Lascaux caves. Lascaux and Bethlehem: one struggle! Perhaps the faithful carry the hymn in their hearts, the hymn to this original reality, this original descent of humanity which they carry to baptismal fonts, but the secret is closely guarded. For outside, terrorism is on the prowl and the police stand by. Only in the shadow of an anti-terrorist crackdown can the God-child be revived.

Watching the president's Christmas message produces this same necropolar, white-mass sensation. Seeing the video broadcast of the Christmas service in the cathedral itself, with these pathetic screens and the young worshippers slumped

---

34. Jean-Marie Cardinal Lustiger, Archbishop of Paris.

around them here and there, you tell yourself that God and religion deserved better. Deserved to die, yes, but not this. However, watching the presidential figure and his sonorous inanity, you tell yourself that here you got what you deserved. Chirac is useless – that goes without saying – but so are we all. The question doesn't even arise whether we're useless because he is, or the other way around. Uselessness of this kind has no origin: it exists immediately, reciprocally; like a shared secret, you savour it implicitly – with its warm bitterness – particularly in these cold snaps, as the very essence of the social bond. Sanctioned by that other interactive uselessness – the uselessness of the screen.

Chirac's uselessness cannot be verified. It could be perhaps, if it were a specific quality – or if he were equal to himself. But, unlike Mitterand, who took himself for Mitterand, Chirac doesn't even see himself as Chirac. He neither takes himself for himself nor for anyone else. He does something or he doesn't. And if the situation dictates, he does the opposite. Political will plays no part, for, the way the political sphere is today, it is not a place of will or representation. And how could Chirac start representing something when there no longer is, among the 'people', any profound will or demand to be represented? No point, for example, discussing the dissolution of the Assembly when it is the people itself that has been dissolved. Or when the people has dissolved itself and goes on dissolving in a perpetual night of the fourth of August, surrendering its privilege of being represented, cancelling itself in its own mass.[35]

Today, as a 'people', we are all worthless and useless, which means there are no representatives or represented any more, but merely 'extras'. We at the grass roots are statistical extras and the 'politicians' are TV extras.

35. On 4 August 1789 the French National Assembly met at 8 p.m. and made sweeping reforms, which were generally represented as putting an end to 'feudal' privilege.

Up to this point, everything is fine. As Brecht said of the beer and the cigar, the fact that Chirac does not in himself exist is harmoniously counterbalanced by the fact that the people no longer is a people. It is simply the end of a fine story, or of history itself – a thing which occurs, to use Rivarol's uncompromising formula, between revolution and the spectacle of revolution. (Rivarol is harsher, arguing that doubtless the people 'had only ever wanted the spectacle of revolution' – but let us at least allow history its historical chance.) With that moment past and gone, we no longer have to deal with history or power exactly (and, even less, with seizing power), but with the fiction and spectacle of power which, for the entertainment of the people, has to feed on the same simulated events as real history (the un-dying – though transparent and nostalgic – image of which still haunts imaginations).

Only those events – strikes, speeches, elections, assassination attempts – which are caught up in their own spectacle exist today. Those involving real issues of representation do not.

Moreover, the characteristic real events (for example, the three which top this year's list: paedophilia, unemployment and mad cow disease) are unrepresentable; they are impossible to pin down politically (even unemployment seems like a viral epidemic or a slow-motion social collapse). Highly symptomatic events, but representative of nothing whatsoever.

Without this – possibly violent – element of spectacle and in the absence of any real issues, everything goes along smoothly, merging in with the normal state of political affairs, which is, as we know, as flat and spongy as an encephalogram. Now, if the fiction and the pleasure of spectacle are to be preserved, a differential tension has to be maintained. As in the story of the illusionist who was forced during his performance artificially to mechanize his gestures to mark himself off from the automaton at his side – an automaton so perfect you could not tell the difference between man and machine. Now, this is precisely what is happening: you cannot distinguish Chirac from the general state of things. He blends in perfectly with the automatic nullity of the state of things. You cannot hold this against him; you can only pity him for it. This is his deepest nature – this basic mimicry, this Rousseauism of a natural landscape gardener of the political scene. But, as a consequence, even in a zero-sum game, he saps all the passion from things. And this is inexcusable. Except that in this extreme corruption – connected with simplicity – by which he, a useless person, becomes the perfect mirror of everyone's uselessness, he might well give all those he (so negatively) represents the idea of smashing the mirror to recover another image – at least in the scattered fragments. And this might be (who knows?) a new form of presence or representation, involving the dispelling of this representative uselessness.

But wouldn't this elimination (and that of many others) still be the *spectacle* of his disappearance? Now, that is something Chirac provides, unaided, on every occasion.

7 January 1997

The Clone or the Degree
Xerox of the Species

Assuredly, the animal world still has some surprises in store for us. After the mad cow, the cloned sheep. Crazy Cow and Baby Dolly. And it is not by chance that together they form the astral theme of this century's end. We are going to be able to clone ever more sheep and so make more and more animal feed with which to feed ever more mad cows . . .

But there is even more of a connection between the two: cloning is itself a form of epidemic, of contagion, of metastasis of the species – of a species in the clutches of identical reproduction and infinite proliferation, beyond sex and death. The key event here is the liquidation of sexual reproduction and, as a result, of any differentiation of – and singular destiny for – the living being. By way, paradoxically, of science and progress, we are now quite simply eradicating the greatest revolution in the history of living beings, the transition from proto-zoan, bacterial, undifferentiated cell-division – the immortality of single-cell organisms – to sexual reproduction and the inalienable death of every individual being, and replacing this with the biological monotony of the earlier state of affairs, the perpetuation of a minimal, undifferentiated life, for which we have perhaps never stopped yearning.

What Freud termed the death drive was simply this dizzying temptation to return to annihilation in the eternal repetition of the Same, to go back beyond the biological revolution of sex, back beyond death. This is ontology become pure tautology, phylogenesis become pure tautogenesis. Whereas living beings have striven for hundreds of millions of years to wrest the same away from the same – to tear themselves free from this kind of primitive entropy and incest – we are working at the disinformation of the species by cancelling differences and manufacturing entropy with information. The very idea of it! With cloning, we are engaged upon a crucial revision of the whole evolution of living beings, and this represents both the technical and scientific triumph of a species and its death by repetition of its own formula.

The paradox of cloning is that it will produce and reproduce beings which are still sexed, whereas the sexual function has become absolutely useless since, just as each segment of earthworm reproduces itself as a whole worm, every cell of a managing director can produce a new managing director (in much the same way as every fragment of a hologram can again become the matrix of the complete hologram).

But this phantasm of repetition is merely one side of the biogenetic enterprise: the other is perfection. For centuries, in the theological debate on resurrection, there was speculation as to which body would be resuscitated. Would it be the body in the full flush of youth, the regenerated, transfigured body, or the old, sick one? This same debate now comes back to us in a bio-industrial version, for it is clear that it won't be the sheep with staggers or the African with AIDS that will be cloned. It is obvious that cloning, if it is to develop, will be automatically discriminatory – far more than natural selection ever was. In this way it will connect with that other phantasm underlying the whole genetic project (the whole technical project in general): the phantasm of perfecting the ideal formula for the species so that nothing remains but to reproduce it. But we have to look at what 'ideal' and 'perfection' mean here. They assume an unrelenting selection in terms of agreed models of race, health, performance and 'intelligence' (defined by operational quotients). Now, this does not raise too many problems where transgenic maize or butchers' meat are concerned, where perfection is a question of what is best to eat. And it does, perhaps, pose no problems for God, since He is the (dis)embodiment of perfection. But where the human species and other complex beings are concerned, the problem is insoluble. Biologically, however, it will be resolved in terms of the weakest formula, that is to say, in terms of perfect normality, unerring adaptation, eradication of all anomalous (or useless) characteristics and genes, and thus, ultimately, in terms of functional and statistical perfection. And in this way, we shall meet the same fate as animals (it is only justice that we should). Immortality and perfection achieved through genetic engineering and cloning will only ever be the immortality and perfection of the average formula, of the 'mediocrity' of the species raised to a higher power.

All this virtual eugenics might perhaps be justified, at a pinch, if the aim were to create a 'higher race' (a higher level of complexity). But all manipulation intended to bring the species closer to normal perfection – or, in other words, statistical mediocrity – is thoroughly abject. Unless there is here, perhaps, some obscure desire to obliterate the specificity of the species by genetic confusion, to change the rules of the game at the risk of coming to grief. In which case, there can be no objection: human beings have always done this in the symbolic order, now they will do it in the biological order. There is, however, an appreciable difference in actually carrying out the biological deed, when this fated character of the Same, which up to now was merely mental or metaphysical, becomes materially inscribed in our cells, and when science itself becomes a 'fatal strategy'. Everyone may at some time have dreamt of duplicating or multiplying himself to perfection, but this is, precisely, a fantasy: it is destroyed when you attempt to force reality to conform to it. Everything – utopias, transparency, perfection – becomes terrifying as soon as it is turned into a reality.

DNA itself, that meta-stabilized formula for life, is perhaps merely an average formula, which has only managed to universalize itself on the basis of a statistical outcome – that is to say, a lowest common denominator. Singularity being, by definition, what can never be reproduced, all that can be reproduced to infinity can only ever be of very low definition.

Multiplication is positive only in our system of accumulation. In the symbolic order, it is equivalent to subtraction. If five men pull on a rope, the force they exert is added together. By contrast, if an individual dies, his death is a considerable event, whereas if a thousand individuals die, the death of each is a thousand times less important. Each of two twins, because he has a double, is ultimately just half an individual – if you clone him to infinity, his value becomes equal to zero.

This is already visible here and now in the social register, where what the system produces and reproduces are virtually matching beings, beings substitutable for each other, already mentally cloned. In the end, this whole cloning business is not so very new; we have experience of it in all areas of life – intellectual, cultural and operational, not to mention the fields of work and technology, where the system long since trained us to be clones of ourselves or of each other. Cloning, the *écriture automatique* of 'ready-made' individuals and their identification with a minimal formula (their mental, behavioural code), their unthinking inscription in the operational networks – all these things are already largely achieved. The clones are already there; the virtual beings are already there. We are all replicants! We are so in the sense that, as in *Blade Runner*, it is already almost impossible to distinguish properly human behaviour from its projection on the screen, from its double in the image and its computerized prostheses.

This is the case in a number of fields. We are familiar with the replica of the Lascaux cave and with Richard Bohringer's cinematic double.[36] But isn't Europe itself, as it is being developed from the top down, a virtual, artificially cloned entity? And isn't virtual reality as a whole an immense cloning of the so-called real world?

Admittedly, with cloning, we are dealing with an infinitely more subtle and artificial prosthesis than any mechanical one. The genetic code, substituting for the father and the mother, becomes the true universal matrix, the individual being now only the cancerous metastasis of his basic formula. Such is the incredible violence of genetic simulation. But this is, at bottom, merely the final phase of a process our modern technologies have simply speeded up: the process of an ideal counterfeiting of the world, allied to the phantasm of an immortal recurrence. In other words, the perfect crime: the work of finishing off the world, for which we now have to undergo a process of mourning. A recurrence which is the exact opposite of Nietzsche's Eternal Return (of the Same). That assumed that things were caught in a necessary, fatal concatenation which exceeded them. Nothing of the kind applies today, where they are caught in a contiguity running off, with no great consequence, to infinity. Today's Eternal Return is the return of the infinitely small, the fractal – the obsessive repetition of things on a microscopic, inhuman

36. Bohringer was the first French actor to provide a voice for a virtual reality 'double' of himself. This virtual 'clone' starred as Dr. Nemo in *20,000 lieues au-delà du réel* (20,000 Leagues beyond the Real), a documentary produced by the Cité des Sciences et de l'Industrie de La Villette.

scale. It is no longer the exaltation of a will, nor the sovereign affirmation of an event, a 'becoming', and its consecration by an immutable sign, as Nietzsche had it. It is the viral recurrence of micro-processes, which is equally ineluctable, but which no powerful sign brings alive in our imaginations.

This is why none of the ethics committees will change anything. With all their good intentions, they are merely the expression of our bad conscience about the irresistible and fundamentally immoral development of our sciences – a development which has brought us to this point and to which we secretly consent, while supplementing that consent with the moral delights of repentance.

Let us say, to console ourselves, that the cloned twin will never be the same as his 'begetter', that he will never be 'as turned into himself by the genetic code',[37] because thousands of complicating factors will make him a different being in spite of everything, but also because there will have been another before him – which is not the case with the original.

And in fact the clone can be seen – this is the positive side of repetition – as the parody of the original, as its ironic, grotesque version, the way Napoleon III was, in Marx's view, the grotesque double of Napoleon I. One can imagine all kinds of new-style conflicts arising from this. Such as the future clone doing away with his 'father', not in order to sleep with his mother (something which is now impossible), but so as to recover his status as original and his exclusive identity. Like the final scene of *Jurassic Park*, where the living dinosaurs, all cloned from fossilized DNA, burst into the dinosaur museum and wreak havoc among their ancestors before being themselves exterminated. Or, alternatively, the disqualified original taking revenge on his clone. For what becomes of the human being

37. In the original French text here, Baudrillard is playing on the first line of Mallarmé's *Tombeau d'Edgar Poe*: 'Tel qu'en Lui-même enfin l'éternité le change'.

when he is pushed out by his own clone and rendered useless? A reserve? A relic? A fossil? A fetish? An art object? There is no immediate end in sight to the conflict between the original and its double, the clash between the real and the virtual.

17 March 1997

Exorcism in Politics or the Conspiracy of Imbeciles

Two situations, each equally critical and irresolvable: the worthlessness of contemporary art; political impotence in the face of Le Pen. There is a trade-off between the two and a resolution by transfusion: powerlessness to mount any political opposition to Le Pen is displaced on to the terrain of culture and the cultural Holy Alliance. So, when it comes to questioning contemporary art, this can be the product only of reactionary and irrational – if not, indeed, fascistic – thinking.

How can one counter this respectful conspiracy of imbeciles? Sadly, nothing can correct this mechanism of intellectual perversion, since it is inspired by bad conscience and the impotence of our 'democratic' elites to resolve both the impasse of art and the political impasse of the struggle against the Front National. The easiest solution is to merge the two problems in the same moralizing vituperation. The real question then becomes: can one not 'open up' the issue in some way, suggest something unusual, irreverent, unconventional or paradoxical without automatically being seen as coming from the extreme Right (which is, it must be said, a homage paid to the extreme Right)? Why has everything moral, conventional and conformist – things which were traditionally on the Right – now gone over to the Left?

A painful revision. Whereas the Right embodied moral values and the Left, by contrast, a certain contradictory historical and political resolve, the Left today, stripped of all political energy, has become a pure court of morality – the embodiment of universal values, the champion of the reign of Virtue and upholder of the antiquated values of the Good and the True – a court before which everyone is answerable but itself. The political illusion of the Left, deep-frozen for twenty years spent in opposition, has turned out, on the Left's gaining power, to be pregnant not with the meaning of history, but with a morality of history. With a morality of Truth, Right and good conscience – the degree zero of politics and even, we may safely say, the lowest point of the genealogy of morals. This moralization of values in which the historical truth of a particular event, the aesthetic quality of a work of art or the scientific pertinence of a particular hypothesis can be judged only in moral terms, is the historical defeat of the Left (and of thought). Even reality, the reality principle, is an article of faith. Question the reality of a war and you'll be condemned for betraying the moral law.

With the Left as lacking in political vitality as the Right, where has politics moved to? The answer is simple: on to the ground of the extreme Right. As Bruno Latour put it very well in *Le Monde*, the only person talking politics in France today is Le Pen. All the others are talking morality or civics; they sound like schoolteachers or instructors, managers or programmers. Le Pen, committed to evil and immorality, snaffles all the political stakes, scoops up all that has been cast aside or positively repressed by the politics of Good and Enlightenment. The more the moral coalition hardens against him – a mark of political impotence – the more political capital he makes out of immorality, out of being the only one on the side of evil. When, in the past, the Right went over to defending moral values and the established order, the Left did not hesitate to defy those same moral values in the name of political ones. It is itself today the victim of such a slide, of such a dereliction: with the Left overtaken by moralism, the repressed political energy necessarily crystallizes else-where – in the enemy camp. And so the Left, by embodying the reign of Virtue, which is also the reign of the greatest hypocrisy, can only fuel Vice.

If Le Pen didn't exist, he'd have to be invented. He it is who delivers us from a whole evil side of ourselves, from the quintessence of all that is worst in us. For this we should rightly anathematize him. But if he disappeared, woe betide us, exposed to all our racist, sexist and nationalist viruses (we all have them) or, quite simply, to the murderous negativity of social being. In this respect he is the mirror of the political class, who use him to exorcize their own evils, just as we use them to exor-cize all the corruption inherent in the operation of society. The same corrupting function, the same cathartic function. The desire to root all this out, the desire to purify society and moralize public life, to liquidate all that represents evil, shows a total misconception of the mechanisms of evil, and thus of the very form of the political.

The anti-Le Pen forces, employing tactics of unilateral condemnation and showing no appreciation of this reversibility of evil, have entirely abandoned its use to Le Pen himself. As a result he is, by his very exclusion, in an impregnable position. The political class, by stigmatizing him in the name of Virtue, puts him in the most comfortable of situations, where all he has to do is sweep up the sym-bolic charge of ambivalence, of rejection of evil and hypocrisy which his righteous adversaries obligingly produce for him – almost as if they were in his pay. He draws his energy from his enemies themselves, who rush to turn his own mistakes to his advantage. They have not understood that good is never the product of rooting out evil, which always exacts a glorious revenge, but of subtly treating evil with evil.

Le Pen is, then, the embodiment of stupidity and worthlessness, admittedly, but of the stupidity and worthlessness of the others, of those who, in denouncing him,

denounce their own impotence and stupidity, simultaneously revealing the absurdity of fighting him head on without any understanding of this diabolical game
of musical chairs – thus, in a terrifying lack of lucidity, feeding up their own phantoms, their own negative doubles.

What governs this perverse effect by which the Left is stuck in denunciation,
while Le Pen retains an exclusive hold on enunciation – with the one profiting fully
from his crime and the other harvesting all the negative effects of recrimination, the
one delighting in evil and the other becoming entangled in victimhood? The
answer is a simple truth: by confining Le Pen to a ghetto, the democratic Left has
walled itself up; it points to itself as the discriminatory power and exiles itself in its
obsession. It automatically cedes the other party's claim of a denial of justice. And
Le Pen does not shy from appealing to Republican legality for his own advantage.
Above all, however, he cloaks himself in the illegal, imaginary, but very profound
prestige of the persecuted – so well, indeed, that he can enjoy the benefits both of
legality and illegality. From this ostracism he derives a freedom of language and a
boldness of judgement which the Left denies itself.

An example of the magical thinking which currently does service for political
thought: Le Pen is criticized for rejecting and excluding immigrants, but this is as
nothing compared with the process of social exclusion which is going forward at
all levels of society (exclusion itself, together with the 'social fracture', found
itself excluded by the decree dissolving the National Assembly). And this complex,
inextricable process of collective responsibility is one we are all accessories to, and
victims of. It is, therefore, typically magical thinking to seek to ward off this
virus which is spreading everywhere as an effect of our social and technical
'progress'; to exorcize this curse of exclusion and our impotence in the face of it
by vesting it in one execrable man, institution or group, whoever or whatever they
may be; to treat it as a canker that could simply be surgically removed, when the

secondary infections have already spread to all parts. The Front National is merely following the paths beaten by these secondaries – paths beaten with all the more virulence for the fact that we believe we have eliminated the tumour, and so, as a result, the germs spread into the whole organism. Not to mention that this magical projection where the Front National is concerned does to *it* precisely what *it* does to immigrants. We must beware of this ruse of contamination in which, by sheer transparence of evil, the positive changes into a negative virus, and the demand for liberty into 'democratic despotism'. As ever, we see here that reversibility, that subtle coiling and winding, of evil which catches rational intelligence off its guard (when the whole of modern pathology teaches us so much about this at the level of the physical body, we pay no heed to it where the social body is concerned).

To remain with politics, we must avoid ideology and see things in terms of social physics. Our democratic society is the stasis and Le Pen the metastasis. Society as a whole is dying of inertia and immunodeficiency. Le Pen is the visible transcription of this viral state, its spectacular projection. Things here are as they are in dreams: he is the burlesque, hallucinatory figuration of this latent state, of this silent inertia made up in equal measure of enforced integration and systematic exclusion. Since, in this society, the hope of reducing social inequality has (almost) definitively disappeared, we should not be surprised to see the resentment shifted on to race inequality. The bankruptcy of the social project is responsible for the successful re-emergence of race (and of all the other forms of fatal strategies). In this sense, Le Pen is the only 'unofficial' analyser of this society. The fact that the analysis is on the extreme Right is merely a sad consequence of the fact that there is no such analyst on the Left or the far Left. And certainly none is to be found among the judges or the intellectuals. Only immigrants, at the opposite extreme, might also be in a position to analyse what is going on, but a certain form of 'right thinking' has largely taken them over. Le Pen is the only one radically to minimize the Right–Left distinction – admittedly, because it is of little importance to him, but the uncompromising critique of that distinction made since the 1960s and in 1968 has unfortunately disappeared from political life. He benefits, then, from a *de facto* situation the political class refuses to face up to (indeed, they do all they can to mask it with elections), but one day the extreme consequences of that situation will have to be drawn. If, one day, political imagination, political will and resolve have some opportunity to bounce back, they will do so only on the basis of the radical abolition of this fossilized distinction which has, over the decades, revealed itself to be an empty sham, and which only holds up now by corrupt collusion. It is a distinction which has vanished in reality, but which, by some incurable revisionism, is constantly being revived, thereby making Le Pen the begetter of the only new political scene. It is as though everyone were involved in scuppering what remains of democracy, doubtless to give the retrospective illusion that it once existed. Many things today have no other existence than this staging of their disappearance. Proving that they existed by a premature act of mourning, Le Pen here being the agent of that work of mourning and the man carrying out the 'contract'.

Is there some chance of drawing the consequences of this extreme (but original) situation other than through the hallucinatory medium of Le Pen – that is to say, other than by a magical conjuration which saps all energies? How are we to avoid succumbing to this viral excrescence of our own demons, other than by going back, beyond political moralism and democratic revisionism, to that unofficial analysis which Le Pen and the Front National have in a sense snatched from us?

7 May 1997